"THE BOX OF PRECIOUS STONES"

by

Alessandro Gigli

A box full of Controversial Poems. Poems about Life, Death, Love and Hate. Poems about Past, Present and Future. Poems about you.

ISBN: 978-1-08-950354-5

About the Author

Hi, my name is Alessandro Gigli, I am a musician, singer, songwriter, music producer and painter based in Kent, England.

To me poetry is the essence of life, the essence of love, the essence of everything. A life lived reading poems I believe is a better life.

I hope you agree with me.

Why I Wrote This Book

This book is a collection of poems that I have written during my entire life and it is part of a series of books of poems that will be released one by one shortly after this one.

I have chosen the best poems from my collection for you and put them in a "BOX."

The title is very personal, because each one of these poems is like a child to me. I called them "Precious Stones."

I hope that you will enjoy reading them.

Why You Should Read This Book

These poems are based on real-life events. Each one of them will give you a strong message. You may find some of the poems, contained in this "BOX," a bit controversial. I believe controversy is important and even essential in this life.

You will also find that these poems, are made by a rebel for rebels like you. Each one of these "Precious Stones" will make you see the world differently; it will show you different perspectives; it will show you beautiful things and ugly things.

The most important thing to do is to use your personal interpretation in order to make these poems yours.

"War makes no men"

War makes no men.

War makes cowards
hiding behind a gun,
a rifle and a bayonet.

War comes in different flavors:
war can be fought by hands;
war can be fought by tanks;
or, war can be fought
by pushing a button,
usually a red button.

Why red?

Must be because red
is the colour of violence,
war and blood.

When the button is pushed,
obliteration of mankind comes.

When war is fought by hands,
instead, could be that a sudden
smile ends the war.

Make no mistake,
war does not make men.

War makes only cowards,
hiding behind a computer,
pushing things
and killing millions.

We should all ask God
to come and collect
weapons,
helmets,
uniforms
and boots
because there will
be no tomorrow
if the big
three starts.

(Thoughts of a soldier on patrol to kill other men)

"Ignorance"

Ignorance is a disease,
a demonic possession
that takes your life,
makes you blind
and makes you think
you are invincible.

Ignorance is a weird
place where you
might be at some
point in your life.

The best weapon
against ignorance
is education.

Anything that improves
yourself is a blessing
and a salvation
from this plague.

Read, save yourself!

"Anger and Oppression"

In this wonderful life,
I am just not able to take
any form of anger and
oppression toward me
or others.

We are born free
and each one of us
is a very special creature.

I love equality;
I love getting up
in the morning
having my heart
at ease and not
feeling as a slave.

Things like anger,
repression, oppression
and jealousy are all symptoms
of a weak and lost mind.

Usually weak minds
get attached to
things that
do not exist,
illusions.

Let go of any attachment
in order to free yourself.

"Possessions"

I believe that
in this life,
we shouldn't
be attached
to anything.

I believe we should
give everything away,
rather than
keeping things.

The more you have,
the less freedom
you have.

I envy
indigenous people
living in
the rain forest
because they live
life on a day
by day basis.

Nature will
provide for them.

They are free
of heavy weights.

"A Different Perspective"

Today I have
looked up
in the sky.

It is amazing to see
how everything
changes among
the clouds.

There is a different
world up there.

You can't get
lost up there
where there are
no roads,
only freedom
and grace.

"Inspiration"

I wake up
every morning in a
peculiar state of mind,
a state of mind
that takes my soul
and my spirit to places;

a state of mind
that makes me write,
pushes my heart forward
and my life forward;

a state of mind
that is persistent
throughout the day.

I ask myself what
is the cause of this?

and the answer is:
the more I grow up,
the more I feel like a kid,
a rascal running free,
a seagull on the
extended ocean.

My existence is my
whole inspiration.

"Failures"

A failure is an
incredible
opportunity
to improve
yourself
therefore is
essential.

But be careful,
don't persevere
in failing.

Learn and
earn something
valuable from
a mistake.

"Failures (Part 2)"

I have always
failed in my life
in any possible way.

This has left an
empty space in me
and made my
mind silent.

But all of the sudden,
I realized that my
failures have turned
into my fortune.

Without failing
I wouldn't
have learnt about
life and how to
be well balanced.

Therefore I am
thankful to whatever
happened to me,
to my past, which
has made me
who I am today,
a much better
person.

"Distance"

Distance means
nothing,
because you
and I are
capable of
feeling each
other through
our minds.

With our thoughts
we send each
other love
and messages
as if we were
telepathic.

Sometimes we
might feel lost
because of the
unbearable
distance
and we might
feel in prison.

But soon we
will have
our reward.

Our reward
will be to be
one forever
and ever.

"Lost Hopes"
A blurred image is like lost hopes.

"Wolf"
I wish I was a lonely wolf sometimes.

"Seagull"
I wish I was a seagull to fly free in the sky, to feel the wind on my face, to feel free and be part of nature.

"Infidelity"
Infidelity is a symptom of insecurity and immaturity.

"Hiding"
Hiding is a symptom of infidelity.

"Around us"
The Universe, the Earth and its ecosystems belong to all of us; If we harm these things, all we are doing is harming ourselves.

"Children"

Life on another planet is something we should consider because we are all children of the Universe.

"Maturity and Nirvana"

Maturity is a gift from God; Maturity is reaching Babylon or Nirvana.

"Lost"

Being lost in life sometimes is normal. It is important to find yourself, but this takes time and effort. You start as being lost and you gradually find yourself in the walk of life.

"Loving forever"

Loving you is like loving forever.

"Love is art"

Love is a serious thing, pure art.

"Love"

Regarding love, If I can't put a smile on your face, then this love will become hate.

"Always right"
Being always right is absolutely wrong!

"The Result of Your Actions"
Whatever happens to you, is the result of your actions.
Keep on adding and never subtracting.

"Tunnel"
Illumination is like exiting a tunnel.

"Long sleep"
Sudden inspiration is like waking up from a long sleep.

"Home made"
There is nothing better than home-made marmalade,
apple pie and cherry pie.

"Her eyes"
The Universe, the ocean, the sky, the mountains, the
rivers and her eyes on me.

"Your kisses"

Your kisses remind me of red Italian tomatoes.

"Water"

There is nothing better than water.

"Believing"

There is nothing better than believing.

"Nature"

There is nothing better than a life lived according to nature.

"Useless things"

There is nothing better than throwing useless things away.

"Self achievement"

Self achievement is giving everything you have away for a good cause.

"Teaching"
Three quarters of teaching is acting.

"Jealousy"
Jealousy is a thing of the past.

"The internet"
The internet is responsible for creating empty spaces and separating people.

"Daughters and sons"
The feeling that one has for a daughter or a son is greater than life itself.

"Milestones"
The Earth with its creatures, is a project. Therefore treasures and things left by ancient civilizations are the Earth's milestones.

"Be real"
The ultimate goal in life is to be real.

"Jealousy (Part 2)"
Jealousy is the devil in person.

"Judging"
Judging someone is a symptom of jealousy.

"Lush life"
A lush life is a pure illusion. I'd rather talk to an animal, swim in open ocean, lay on the grass for hours or climb a mountain.

"Security and stability"
Security and stability are feelings that come with time; the journey to get there might be difficult.

"Insecurity"
Insecurity is a symptom of inferiority.

"Inferiority"
A lush life is a symptom of inferiority.

"Lust"
Lust is something we should not be interested in.

"Love, purity, and grace"
If I judge, then I am against love, purity and grace.

"Mercy"
Love for a child shows mercy.

"Love for an animal"
Love for an animal means that one has a good heart.

"Gravity"
The true meaning of things is to be found in outer space at zero gravity (Picture this.)

"Predators"
Predators are fascinating and perfect machines, nature's bizarre inventions.

"Coral reef"
If love is a coral reef, then I am a predator hiding in it.

"Zoo"
If love is a zoo, then we are the wild beasts in it.

"Fisherman"
If love arrives suddenly, then I am a fisherman waiting patiently.

"Desert storm"
If love is a desert, then we are a desert storm.

"It's all good"
Love is saying: 'it's all good'.

"Made of love"
Love is what we are made of.

"Get rid of it or embrace it"

Regarding love, I wish I could get rid of it! Or lose myself in it.

"Get it right"

Regarding love, I wish I could get it right.

"Delicate and hard"

Love can be delicate as a flower or hard as a stone.

"Perpetual machine"

Love is a perpetual machine. Once it starts it will never stop unless a disaster occurs.

"What is love"

Is love a goal? An abstract thing? A wild beast?

"Desert island"

Love is a desert island.

"Pushing heart"
Love is my heart pushing forward.

"An attitude"
Love is an attitude.

"Things happen"
If things happen for a reason, then tell me the reason
why I have lost you.

"Kids"
Kids are the essence of life, a new beginning, the re-
engineering of the world.

"Knowing"
If I only knew it before.

"Flame"
The flame lit within us, is our soul responding and
reacting to the events of this world.

"Children are us"

Children are the continuity of ourselves therefore they are us in every sense.

"Give it away"

Happiness is giving everything you have away.

"Divine intervention"

Friendship is a gift from above, a divine intervention.

"Compassion"

Compassion is a virtue, a gift.

"We do exist"

If life is not an illusion, then it's true we do exist!

"Formality"

Differences between two languages are only a formality.

"Race"

Being at the same level is understanding that there are no races in this world.

"Patterns"

Nature is sublime when it combines colours, patterns and shapes never seen together before.

"Nature"

If Nature is a lady, then I am in love.

"Material things"

Material things are evil, diabolical and not of this world.

"Giving"

Giving makes one remembered.

"Changes"

Changes make me supernatural, invincible and eternal.

"Mercy (Part 2)"
Mercy is a pillar of our life.

"Challenges"
Challenges make me invincible.

"Mirror"
The real nature of things is a mirror.

"The divine ignition"
God has ignited life, but nature took over and started the evolution process.

"Simplicity"
Simplicity is a sign of maturity.

"Facing a challenge"
When facing a challenge, do not face it as a loser, but face it as a winner, like a roaring lion and running forward.

"Hitler"
If only he would have been given a chance as an artist.

"Patriotism, Nationalism"
Nationalism is a form of Patriotism Extremism.

"Ambition"
Too much ambition will kill you.

"The Mission"
Life is a mission from beginning to end and the pay-day is right at the end.

"Achieve"
Achieve happiness in any possible legal way!

"Problems"
Problems are a daily routine!

"Wisdom"
Achieve wisdom in any possible legal way!

"Sky"
Fly high in the sky with your mind!

"Getting there"
Get there in any possible legal way!

"Out of the body"
Have an out of the body experience for once!

"The best of you"
Give the best of you, but don't give it away for free!

"My life"
My life is my muse.

"Be proud"

Be proud of paying for your mistakes.

"Details"

Do every little thing and don't miss anything.

"Pathology"

Being obsessed with someone is not like being in love, it's a pathology.

"Colours"

No matter what colour you are, I'm with you.

"Getting better"

I always wonder if it will get better.

"Competing"

I don't compete, I don't impress, I'm just me.

"Solitude and silence"
Solitude is sublime and silence is full of sound and harmony.

"Uncertainty"
The only certain thing in this life is uncertainty.

"The worst and the best"
The worst things that happen to us are the best things.

"The storm"
There is a storm at sea, just like in my heart. The storm will never end.

"Unison"
In unison we suffer; in unison we succeed; there is no life without a system made of things, objects and people; There is never a separation, never a dissonance.

"Walking in these empty streets"

It seems
like Winter,
even though
it is Spring.

The sky is dark,
the wind blows
on my face
and its raining.

Streets are empty,
endless
and I walk
without a direction,
with sadness
in my heart
and the hope
to change.

"The Seagull"

Fly Seagull fly free,
upon this endless coast,
upon endless oceans.

Adrenaline is your only friend,
while you come down hard
and U-turn suddenly.

I would give an arm
to feel what you feel;
I would give an arm
to be you.

Lucky you Seagull,
you are free.

Lucky you Seagull,
you breath pure air
up there.

You are even closer to the sun.

Your friends are the Sunrise
and the Sunset.

You don't know what the future is,
you don't care about it.

You live day by day,
while we, down here,
are just dust in the wind
living on hopes.

We, Humans, admire you
and write about you.

Lucky you Seagull,
you live your life
questions free.

"The Boat"

I am walking on the coast,
early in the morning.

The wind embraces me,
while I walk.

On the line of the horizon
I can see a silhouette,
a black outline.

The silhouette is a boat
which gets closer and closer,
brought to shore by
the current of the ocean.

There is no one on board.

It's getting closer
and closer to shore;
I can touch it now.

Its surface is rough,
beaten by the ocean's weather.

While I touch it,
I can imagine the places
this boat has been.

This boat reminds
me of ourselves
lost in oceans of people.

"We are connected"

At 5 am I walk alone in an
endless street of solitude.

At a crossroad,
another man
walks toward me.

It's 5 am and no one is around,
just myself and this man,
at the same crossroad,
at the same time
and at the same location.

We are connected,
it is a thing of life.

There is an energy in the
air that allows us to connect.

Every time we
reach a crossroad,
every time we reach
the end of a block,
there is another person doing
exactly the same thing.

"Marilyn Monroe"

It is true that
Gentlemen
prefer blondes,
the blondes
of Los Angeles
and a Martini
on Sunset Blvd.

As a sex symbol
you were the one.

As an icon
you are the one.

Marilyn from up there.

Now that you've
arrived at this bus stop,
in a bus full of misfits,
please tell us...

Were you murdered?

Or is it true that you
have committed
suicide?

"Secret place"

There is a secret place
I want to take you.

Only you have
access to this
secret place.

The secret place is
in my chest.

It is my heart.

"Mother Teresa"

Mother Teresa
the Albanian
crossing mountains
and rivers,
did to the
Catholic Church,
what no other
has ever done.

An illustrious
career in poverty,
a resume in charity,
a unique curriculum
indeed.

But voices run wild
as well as conspiracies.

Rumors exist about
things happened
in the far
away Calcutta
that could
ignite controversy.

Little secrets
that Mother Teresa
holds in her resting
place forever.

Villain or hero
she obtained
canonization.

She is a saint,
for many
a saint with a twist.

"Dead tree"

There is a broken
branch in the field.

Only a fractured
branch is left.

No trees,
no birds,
no butterfly,
no flowers.

Just a lonely
and broken stick.

"Night"

Night is like colouring
a white sheet
with the colour black.

Night is like
turning off all lights.

Night is like saying
that the day is over.

If the meaning
of Night is the end of things,
then I'm the King of this
endless night.

"What matters"

If I run for my life,
it is because
life is precious.

If I run for you,
it is because
you are precious.

What really matters
makes you move.

"Tsunami"

Love is an
endless waltz,
an endless roller-coaster,
an interminable storm,
a Tsunami.

"Empathy"

I have grown up
understanding others.

I have always placed
myself into someone
else's shoes.

What a shame.

No one has ever
understood me.

"Generosity"

Someone thinks that
generosity is a crime.

As a matter of fact,
you should never
give anything to anyone.

Just keep it for your self.

That's what they think.

This is humanity.

I want to give
everything away
just like San Francesco did.

It has been proved
that giving is receiving.

The person who
does not give,
shall never receive.

Greed is bad,
desire is dark,
like the darkest
winter night
with a blizzard.

"Loneliness"

Loneliness is my
companion for life.

Once you're alone,
you will never go back.

Loneliness is
like a prison,
once you enter,
the key to
your cell is thrown
away forever.

"Regarding love again"

Few more verses
dedicated to love,
this time wrote
in black ink,
as if this was
a funeral.

Sometimes,
love reaches the
point of no return;

an abyss with very
slippery walls.

In black ink
these verses are written,
because black is the
colour of the end.

"The loved ones"

My loved ones
are far away.

We are in a triangle,
like the Bermuda Triangle.

A triangle of love,
hate,
indifference
and sudden scares.

Unknown forces interrupt
our communication always.

My loved ones,
do love me,
but oceans
and bad weather
separate all of us,
just like in an
eternal despair.

"You"

You...it's just a word,
but not for me.

You...it's just you.

You're special,
you're kind,
you're different,
you're caring.

My life,
the moon
and the stars
exist around you.

You...you are everything
I could ever have.

You...you're everything
I could ever dream.

My heart,
my soul,
my words,
all for you.

You're my first love,
my best life lesson to have.

"The human part of things"

The human
part of everything,
is always more
complicated then
the problem itself.

As a matter of fact
to solve a problem,
man is capable of
creating an
infinite number
of smaller or
bigger problems
around it.

"Forever"

Forever and ever
you and I,
together forever.

When the
night comes,
you will be
my shelter.

You love me
and I love you.

Alone,
alone with you,
we understand
each other,
we care about
each other.

And if the night
will be cold,
I will be your shelter.

If the night
will be dark,
I will be your
guide.

"I don't understand"

I don't understand,
you said you loved me
but you don't.

I don't understand,
why the world
goes as it goes.

I don't understand,
why things get strange
and I don't understand,
why friends come and go.

I don't understand,
why you don't
come as you are.

I don't understand,
why is it taking so long.

I don't really know,
if this is America
or just an empty
space in my heart.

"Spirit"

You're wonderful,
you're a beautiful
spirit in this world.

You're impossible,
but still a beautiful spirit in this world.

Tell me what you're thinking,
when I'm not with you;

tell me what you're feeling,
when I'm not close to you
and when I leave you all alone.

You're so absurd,
the richest person in this world.

You're a dream to me,
a beautiful spirit in this world.

If I follow you,
would you follow me?

If I call your name,
would you call my name?

All I want to be is what you are,
a beautiful spirit in this world.

You're impossible
but still a beautiful spirit in
this world.

"The point of no return"

The space
between two points,
A and B,
represents the whole
pitch-black Universe.

In this space
everything exists,
including you and I.

Between A and B
there are other points:
microscopic moments
of reality,
silence.

At this very moment,
within this entire
majestic suspended animation,
among the stars
and within this
stop-motion effect,
you and I
are at the
point of no
return.

"Charles Darwin"

Darwin came up
with the Theory
of Evolution,
based on Natural
Selection and
the Survival
of the Fittest.

This theory
has shaped
the Modern World.

Because of this theory
the world is sick.

"Who created the Universe?"

Has the Universe
always existed?

Was the Universe
created many
billions of years
ago by unknown
forces or by God?

Just leave the
answers to
personal
interpretation
and imagination.

With imagination
a man has
no boundaries,
just like the Universe.

Imagination
allows one to
float in space and time;

it allows us to create our
own Universe.

"Your Energy"

I will feel
your energy;

in my soul
I will feel it.

I will be born again
in your energy.

Please stay here
inside my heart.

I still try
to live without you.

This feeling is
stronger than me
and you know it.

I will feel
your absence
in every
moment of
my existence.

The Energy
of your body,
is a vital fluid
for my creed.

"You are the best in the world"

Only you,
you're the best
at what you do.

You love me,
that's the very best
 you can do.

And when
the morning comes
in our room
the first thing
you look at is me;
you feel my skin;
you feel my heart;
while I sleep
you gently kiss my lips
and then my eyes.

You put your
hand on my
chest to feel
the sound
of my soul.

Then I wake up;
my eyes into your eyes;
my hand through your hair;
you're the best in the world.

No words can explain
this love I have for you;
the state of mind I'm in;

you're the best in the world.

True love can't be measured;
true love is not a joke;
true love exists at least
between you and me.

"You're special"

You're special to me,
so special to me.

I'm sorry,
for not telling you
how much I've loved you.

I'm sorry,
but I've been busy with life.

All the things you taught me,
will stay with me for life.

All the things you
said and have done,
will stay with me for life.

The other day I found a letter
in a drawer,
it belongs to you and me,
sealed forever and ever.

"Solitude"

I did not ask for this solitude,
even though sometimes
it is so sublime on my skin.

I did not ask for your company,
even though your
company is as essential
as drinking water
in the Sahara desert at midday.

Solitude is like a big fat woman,
shouting words without sound.

Loneliness is like a big fat cat,
sleeping 20 hours per day
and waking up only to eat.

Solitude is like a flag,
a flag coloured only
with one colour,
the colour of pitch black.

I did not ask for this,
but I was given solitude;
I was given a ghost as a lover.

Solitude is a silent ghost of war,
the war of life,
our inner conflict.

"Life is sinister"

What a sinister
thing life is.

There are traps all
over our path of life.

Fake news
and people that are
used to wearing masks,
made of bloody skins.

Life is the real
horror show.

"We are in an atomic era"

The big 3
looms upon us,
in the news,
in newspapers.

I wish the atomic winter
would come to clear up
what humans have done
to this beautiful
blue marble planet.

I know it is cruel to say,
but cruelty is actually
at the foundation of humanity
therefore eye for an eye,
tooth for a tooth.

"Storm Kathy"

Storm Kathy is
coming this way.

I am anxious to
experience its power.

I hope it'll blow me away,
a thousand miles from here,
where I can be real.

Where I can be a man
or an animal of the land.

"A new brain"

I am a human
or perhaps an animal
of this beautiful land.

As an animal
cruelty,
greed
and killing are
things of every day.

One day will come,
when we,
the animals,
will be given
a new brain
and a new
sense for life.

We are still
not quite there yet.

"Love the pulsating beast"

Even though I detest love,
I can't stay away from it.

Yet more sentences
dedicated to this
thing come up,
about this
abstract concept.

Love is a
pulsating beast,
a very wild and
dangerous animal,
which has taught
me to survive.

I'm a survivor,
I survived the beast.

This beast has
a large mouth,
huge fangs
and it is thirsty
for blood.

That's what love is all about.

"Horizon"

The sea,
the sky,
the sun all merge
at a point in
time and space.

They all have
a nice chat
when they
meet at the
line of the
horizon.

"Dirt"

A carrot,
a potato
nurtured
by the same dirt,
picked up
by the
same rough
hands.

"Tomorrow"

Future,
aging
and uncertainty.

Three big things
of tomorrow.

At a certain point,
they become
friends with
lady death.

"Missing seconds"

Lost chances,
opportunities
and missed trains.

All happened
because we
arrived at point B
a few seconds late.

"More about the lifeless love"

Love has no shape,
love is a thing,
love is when you
kick me out
of your house.

Love is lifeless
and it can kill
in a million
different ways.

"Falling star"
Today is a day in which I think of my future and my future is as bright as a falling star.

"Words"
Words come out of her mouth like meat from a meat grinder.

"Crystals"
This relationship is as strong as a crystal that breaks in millions of fragments.

"Devoted"
I am devoted to you as I am devoted to Krishna or Tlaloc.

"Cheetah"
I run in these fields and I'm free as a Cheetah.

"Man from the stars"

I am floating on
the bottomless ocean,
all of the a sudden
I swim in space,
I am no longer human,
I am a man from outer space,
made of stars,
interplanetary.

"In a cage"

I feel like
I'm in a cage.

I have attempted
escaping,
but I can't.

I'm trapped even
in my dreams
and all I can
do is to run
away with my mind.

With my
mind I reach
places not even the
Hubble telescope
has reached.

"Andromeda"

I'm Andromeda,
you are the Milky Way.

We will collide
within a few
billion years.

We will become one
big Galaxy.

Patience my dear,
patience.

"Fibro Fog"

In those moments
in which Fibro Fog
embraces my brain,
I feel the other
dimension,
I feel free,
I feel like I
owe nothing,
I feel like I have
no commitments.

Sometimes
knowing too much
hurts.

"Enigma Machine"

Sometimes
to me you are
the real
unbreakable
Enigma machine.

You talk in ciphers,
you act weird.

I'm not the bomb,
I cannot decipher you.

"Meadows and the big 3"

These verses
are for when
the big 3 will start;

when these
green meadows
will be gone.

To future
generations:
do not play
with the matches.

"Nudity"

Nudity
is not pornography.

A beautiful body
has nothing to do
with vulgarity
nor profanity
and not even crudity.

Nudity is grace.

I can spend hours
looking at you
naked in bed.

I don't even
have to touch.

"Beauty"

Great Beauty
comes with
a high price,
not because
you need
to change
your looks,
but because
beauty is
artistry
and grace,
delicacy
and charm,
elegance
and adorableness.

Beauty is just
a lot of you.

"Poets are fat"

Poets are fat,
indulging in free dreams
and in free food.

"Ladies lie"

Ladies lie, cry;
ladies wear tights
and kill at night.

"The trap"

In the spider's web,
a lonely fly is trapped;
there's no way out of here.

"Lonely place"

The rich man's mansion,
is a more lonely place
than my log cabin
in the Taiga.

"Frog"
The frog jumped
and the ladies started
screaming like babies.

"Discipline"
Discipline is what
undisciplined kids need
to be self-controlled.

"Flower needs water"
I need your love
more than a flower needs
water in summer.

"The Black Birds"

Beware of the
black birds.

In groups
they arrive;
roaming upon
our heads;
dreaming of
stealing jewels
silently
and quietly.

"Social Killer"

Mercy is asked
when facing
a killer,
a psychopath,
a sociopath.

So many die
in the hands
of social killers.

A new type of
serial killer,
a controlling
kind of individuals
robbing us of our life.

They are no more serial,
they are social.

"Eternal"

Death is a
state of mind;
death is not
the end any more.

In this new world
of tomorrow,
artificial intelligence
has replaced life.

Tomorrow is today,
yesterday is hard
to remember
and life is eternal.

"Grace"

I would have loved
to be brought up
running free,
with grace
and no heavy
weights.

"Devotion"

Devotion,
in this eternal
embrace of affection,
is a very powerful thing.

Of all the things
I love in life,
you are the thing
that I cherish the most
and when I'm in trouble
I look for you,
I find light,
I can see everything
and nothing seems
scary any more.

"Horror"

I have hate
in my heart.

I have an
objection
in my soul.

I yearn for war,
nasty looks
and disgust.

The real horrors
of our existence,
are contained
in this box,
in my thorax.

"Mnemonics"

My memory retention
doesn't allow me to
remember our time.

It seems like I'm a machine.

Part of my memory
and knowledge,
have been erased forever,
particularly the one
in which you belong.

All of a sudden
you're gone,
like erased files.

"Mercy (Part 3)"

God have
mercy on me.

I tried hard,
I cried hard.

I yearn for a
new beginning.

"Humanity"

We, the humans,
are unrecognizable
to ourselves.

There's a malevolent
and scary angel
among all of us.

This angel's intentions
are not good.

His intentions
are cruel
and you are a
victim of society
and humanity.

"Social"

We are
social beasts;
we became
social killers,
not serial.

Our hearts are
contaminated
by an invisible
dark force,
that makes
us selfish;
a force that
makes sense
of lunacy.

"Imbalance"

Our life is balanced by events
that shape our present and future.

Our life belongs now to
the madness of technology.

There is an imbalance
between reality and fiction
and therefore among the
various parallel universes.

Every day we fall and
we struggle to create balance.

We become emotional
and fall into the
abyss of social media.

"How much more about love?"

I find myself in a dark corner,
yet again on my lips
the taste of love.

It feels as if someone died,
I'm a mourner and I'm tired,
10 matches to go
and still wearing boxing gloves.

I think about today
and lots of things come to my mind,
I look down, on the carpet,
the same spot where we kissed,
I can't remember
what document I signed.

My memory is gone,
all around my head,
there is a mist.

All this confusion,
is the state that love puts you in.

I swear, I will never do it again.

"Courage"

In life,
you need an
overdose of audacity,
in order to face
the roaring devil.

It all comes down
to your mental capacity.

Be brave,
be daring,
face the beast,
the demons.

When all hope is lost
and you reach
the empty bottom,
It will feel
like a holocaust,
It will feel
like autumn.

You need
to face the Beast,
grab it by its horns,
no need to call a priest,
no need to wear
a crown of thorns.

Face the animal in you,
calm the animal in you.

"For my lover"

For my lover,
I would do
crazy things,
you wouldn't do.

For my lover,
I would carry
on my shoulder
heavy weights.

For my lover,
I would walk
1000 miles,
bare foot.

For my lover,
I would dream
a dream of
only us two.

"Concert Hall"

People running,
jumping
and drinking.

They worship
the stage,
like the earth
longs for an
asteroid.

Gravity
grabs them
and pulls
them in.

The sound
and noise are
diabolical.

Until it feels like being
in an old cemetery,
with 300 years old tombs.

The only sounds come
from rats' teeth,
when the show is over.

"Ants Colony"

Ants march
in distinct patterns.

Scouts walk very far away
from the colony
while soldiers protect the workers.

This is organized chaos,
nature's best engineering opera.

Things work so fine,
like a sausage factory.

They talk to each other
via chemicals in the air.

The only sounds is
the sound of their tiny legs.

They grab all sorts of things,
walk miles,
then into the colony,
down underground,
deep in the soil,
within massive and
complex tunnels,
finally arriving at
the queen's chamber.

What a day!

"Life"

Be attached to life,
not for its
monetary value,
but for its
spiritual and
mystical
significance.

"Death"

She can come
at any given moment.

She is the real
lady in black.

Too skinny
for my taste.

"Coincidence"

It must be a
coincidence or a
glitch in the matrix,
that I met you on
this day.

Or could love
be responsible
for this?

"The Matrix"

In this so-called
cyber era
and fast-paced
society,
all has been
lost to segments
of code;

programming
languages.

"Ghost"

My house is haunted,
but I'm not afraid
as I should be afraid
of the living.

"More on devotion"

Devotion means,
carrying a very
heavy weight,
through a boiling
hot desert.

Devotion means,
swimming above
the Mariana Trench,
without fear of
unknown deep
creatures.

Devotion is not
for everyone.

"Himalayas"

I'm on the summit
of Mount Everest,
in search of Yeti,
in search of myself.

I have been lost since
I was living in a big city.

Now I'm free
and searching;

I'm hungry again.

My hunger
brought me here,
on the summit
of one of the highest
peaks in the world.

Next,
I will reach
the summit of
Olympus Mons.

"Cerberus"

You remind me
of Cerberus,
the dog with
many heads,
guardian of the
underworld,
preventing the
dead from leaving.

You just won't let me go.

"Tlaloc"

The sacred
God of rain,
fertility
and water,
is asking for
sacrifices,
otherwise
he will send hail,
thunder
and storms.

This is how
I would describe
my emotions today.

"Snowflakes"

Snowflakes are falling
from the sky,
more numerous,
minute
after minute.

If you closely look
at each one of them,
they hide a secret
geometry set by God.

Their geometry
is perfection,
too perfect to
be spontaneous,
too perfect to
be so perfect.

"Stay away from love"

Love used to be
contagious like a good vibe.

Love used to be immaculate,
sacred.

The illness called Time,
has changed love
forever.

"Debts"

Debts are vile,
debts are strong,
debts are here to stay.

Sometimes a man
struggles with
paying his debts
because debts are traps.

Traps are for the weak
and have to be paid
every other week.

Debts start by gently
embracing you
and finish with
the kiss of death.

"Marriage"

For me it is just too late,
I will not be able to repent.

I have been married
now several times,
I am already in purgatory,
almost in hell.

Marriages for me
were a death wish.

I have lost everything
even my dignity
and all of my daughters.

I would do it again.

"Traps"

By the time
you get out
of your home,
you realize
that this world is full
of traps.

The financial trap,
the love trap,
the friendship trap,
the dreams trap
and so on.

Today I give
everything away,
today I move
to the mountains.

"Contagious love"

Your love is so precious,
your love is so real,
your love is contagious.

Your love is all I need,
my arms around you,
your love is prestigious.

Contagious as a virus
or as a final kiss.

Contagious as ice cream
in the middle of the Gobi Desert
or as the bite of a viper.

Love started as a simple,
graceful thing
and it ended up by
being a contagious thing.

"Kissing"

Kiss me has you
never did before.

Kiss me like this
was your very first kiss.

Kiss me has this
would be our
last day on earth.

"Tragedy"

Today was perfect,
I went to work,
I had a wonderful,
busy and productive day.

I was able to finish
the day a bit earlier.

I got into my car,
I stopped at a flower shop
and I bought a bunch of red roses,
red as the wine I thought.

I then stopped to buy
a box of chocolate.

Perfection I thought.

I went back home,
I opened the door.

I immediately saw
a few odd things.

Shoes I did not recognize,
a jacket on the sofa I did not recognize.

My face expression changed;
I run upstairs quietly;
I opened the door.

What a show in front of my eyes!

My entire life passed by just like a movie.

I felt like I could fly almost.

Months passed by,
the pain is still just too much.

I can't stop thinking about
my 9mm and then Eureka.

BOOM!

"War"

What is war?
Why do men go to war?
Why do governments
spend so much money
on wars?

War is a business,
it is the business of death,
the industry of depression and tragedy.

It is also the business of stupidity.

We are so capable of
even going to the moon,
but on the other hand
we are just too emotional.

War is the business of greed.

War does not care about our kids.

War does not care about the future.

War cares about how many men die,
including women and kids.

"Climb"
Once reached the highest summit, you need to keep on going up.

"Seek the light"
There is no light in laziness.

"Waiting"
Patience is for the brave. Be brave and get in line.

"Perspectives"

You are ugly
and you are beautiful.

It is all down to
your perspectives.

Therefore
it is not necessary
to listen to
third-party commentary.

Listen only to the
commentary of
your heart
and soul.

"Love Retirement"

Today I have retired
from this foolish
game called love
and if love is the
seventh wave,
then I am Poseidon.

"You scare me"

You are perfectly fine
unless I say something.

You suddenly
turn into the beast,
the demon on earth,
the chupacabras.

It is not possible
to calm you down,
not even if I give you honey,
not even if I give you sugar.

You come right at me,
with all you got.

And even though
you are so strong,
in reality,
you are so weak.

"A gun in my hand"

It is so bizarre,
what a difference
can a gun make,
when held in your hand.

Do I feel like the king in charge?

Do I feel like I can
take on the whole world?

So many different
questions and emotions,
go through my mind,
while holding this
9mm semi-automatic Beretta.

What to do?
How to act?
Should I put it down?

Or should I put a
bullet in someone's head?

"Sold my Soul"

It is 3 am,
I am at this
remote crossroad.

I met with a stranger.

I gave him my soul,
to get rich quickly.

Good music to
the ears of the
chief commander.

Bad music for
the believers,
the resistance.

"Identity theft"

The so-called
technology advances
are responsible
for stealing identities.

Today,
I am not myself any more,
today I fake my happiness,
I fake my future,
I fake my wealth,
I fake my values,
I fake my health,
I fake pretty much
everything a man
can possibly fake.

People are made of plastic
and the struggle of the fittest
is set by whoever has more likes.

What are you willing
to do to have more likes?

Not even this so-called struggle
is genuine any more.

It can only get worst.

"Bank Robbery"

I am watching the news,
there was a bank
robbery in my town.

There was a
bank robbery,
at my bank.

My entire
life savings, gone.

My woman, gone.

My house,
and possessions, gone.

This robbery has been
the bank theft of my life.

"Good with words"

I was told,
that I am good
with words.

I was told,
that I can
tell stories.

It is not me,
it is the angels above,
that are randomly sending
material on earth.

I'm only an angler,
fishing for the big fish.

"The Dynamics of Love"

Even though love
seems to be
completely random,
beautiful, ugly,
predictable, unpredictable,
it has dynamics and laws.

Only a mature heart
is going to be able to
handle the laws and
dynamics of love.

While this heart
is still young,
it will have to deal with,
falling bridges,
breaking roads
and long cold nights.

Therefore I say
that knowing
the dynamics of love,
comes all down
to either avoiding love
all together
or embracing romance
with a degree in
engineering.

"From Zero to Hero"

You get from zero to hero
if you help an old lady
crossing the roads,
if you give away all
of your possessions,
if you buy gifts
for your beloved,
if you face life with a smile,
if you raise a family,
if you play with your kids,
if you learn the dynamics of life,
if you learn the dynamics of love
and if you master the laws of God.

"The amazing Black Cat"

After 11 years of joy,
you are still here.

You are still meowing
outside the door,
so that I can let you in.

I wonder,
what's in your heart for me.

They say that cats are
just diplomatic animals.

Selfish and cold as sharks.

I say differently.

Within these years you
have given me love,
I have given you bawls of
salty disgusting food,
you did not care,
you've always loved me.

After all these years,
we have both got older
and now I feel sorry
and sad cause I sense that
soon you will be gone.

Cats only live about 15 years,
with a bit of luck about 18.

I pray the lord to have
that luck and honor
to have you for has
many years as possible.

While you are here
and while I am here,
let's just love each other.

I will always remember you
like the fantastic Black Cat.

"The Inevitable gift"

There is one thing
at the end of this madness,
there is only one
thing awaiting us
from the moment
that we are born,
she awaits us.

Is it a myth?
An urban legend?

She might be real,
perhaps not has a legend,
but biologically she is.

So after all the troubles
we went through in life,
at the end,
we will get
the inevitable gift.

"Death is Complicated"

What is death?
Is it the end of everything?
What is everything?
Is everything what we see?
What we have? Possess?
If life is a complicated process,
I suppose Death must be
another complicated process.

Is it a biological process?
Or is it Divine intervention?

I am not afraid of facing
this complicated process.

I wish I could understand it.

I wish I would know what lies after death.

Death is for sure a shocking thing,
it starts right at the beginning
and through aging.

Death takes everything
away from us
day after day,
hour after hour,
minutes after minutes,
second after second.

"Clown Syndrome"

Today,
in this society
of images, videos
and most importantly
in this society
based on "Likes,"
a new syndrome
has arisen:
the "Clown Syndrome."

This new disease
of the brain,
makes one believe
to be invincible,
never ridiculous
and always likable.

Some patients of
the clown syndrome,
are capable of doing things
a dog or cat would not do,
just for a few more likes
on their profiles.

The clown syndrome
is the new disease of
the century.

"Syzygy"

In a straight line,
as if they were
coloured marbles,
the sun,
the moon and earth are
lined up for a few moments.

An Eclipse obscures
our life today,
It is a rare event,
an extraordinary event,
so special that I've asked
my girlfriend to marry me
and she said yes.

"Kuiper Belt"

Remnants of events happened
billions of years ago
form the Kuiper Belt.

Far away,
beyond Neptune
and considered to be
the outer rim of
our solar system,
the Kuiper Belt,
is a desolate place
made of ice,
stones
and dust.

It's circular shape
moves forward
in eternity.

A puzzle of stones
perfectly positioned
in this belt built by God.

I try to imagine
what's beyond
this giant circle,
in outer space
and what
comes to
my mind
is desolation
and spaces
so immense,

that our ant's brain
will never comprehend.

This is why we are
humans and God is God.

There is a big difference.

"Cheap and made of plastic"

This love
is cheap and made
of plastic.

This love is a scam.

This love,
made me believe,
that the world
was mine,
when it wasn't.

This love is
a maniac,
a psychopath,
a sociopath
and it's cheap
and made
of fragile,
breakable,
thin plastic.

"Roaring T-Rex"

Tyrannosaurus,
what a beautiful name.

The Rex,
the King of his dominions.

When Laramidia disappeared,
you were also gone,
into ashes,
into the wind,
preserved for eternity.

66 million years ago,
due to an event
during the Cretaceous,
a phenomenon called
the Tertiary Extinction,
made you a legend
Ad Infinitum.

Today,
you are still
misunderstood for
what you were,
a perfect,
complex,
gracious
and unique
natural machine.

"The observer"

I stand here,
surrounded by everything
and everyone.

I watch life and lifeless things
passing by.

I'm the observer,
the big brother,
who does not stand
here to judge,
who does not
stand here to criticize.

Things go this way,
because they
are meant to be this way.

I will always be here,
without moving,
just watching.

I will instead be an outsider,
an outcast,
a hermit.

I rather fly to Mars
with my imagination,
then getting involved.

I watch,
I learn,
I pray

and meditate.

I'm the mountain
upon the valley,
where fertile grounds
give birth to fruits.

I'm like a god.

"Surfing on your curves"

We are in a dark room,
lights on you only,
on your naked curvy body.

I'm seating in front of you,
while the photographer
prepares his cameras.

With one arm you cover
your breasts,
with one hand
you cover your "Butterfly."

My imagination runs wild.

You're now laying down,
I'm on a snowboard,
I start from your heap,
and slide down to your side,
then on your breasts and nipples.

I slide down
all the way to your
Butterfly and I rest
there for a while.

"Reaching the infinite"

I've entered
a rotating tube,
a giant rotating
endless passage
with moving walls.

They move and
melt into a spiral.

I'm a bit confused,
but I walk forward
into the spiral,
as I am attracted
to voices and to
a very intense
white light.

Its God's light,
the light of
the infinite.

"Getting much older"

It's a fact,
I'm getting older.

I walk the same
streets I used
to walk on,
when I was a little kid.

I look at the same sky
I used to look at,
when I was a little kid.

There's Mars
and there's the Moon.

They haven't changed,
not even a bit.

I have changed.

I went from caterpillar
to adult butterfly.

I wonder what's next.

"Astrometry"

The astrometric
measurements to
Kepler-62f,
will lead me to
eternity.

I'm off,
to an interplanetary
one way trip.

I might become
dust while the
trip takes place,
but eventually
my particles
will arrive to
destination.

Particles might
live forever
and colonize
Kepler.

All the evolved
living beings,
will be my
children.

"Panspermia"

Last man,
first man.

It all depends on Panspermia.

Our genetic heritage,
according to bio-ethics,
has to become interplanetary.

The problem is interstellar transit.

How to achieve it?
Is this only a dream?
Is this the way we were brought
to our planet four billion years ago?
I'd love to send my DNA to Alpha Psa
or Beta Pictoris.

How amazing this would be?

It could be like being there.

I can picture myself,
floating in a protoplanetary
cloud or orbiting around
a brand new planet in a habitable zone.

I just need to make sure
to have a high probability
to be captured
by a celestial being's
gravitational pull.

Since we are not
able to discover life
outside our Milky Way,
it makes sense
to expand humanity
by seeding
other far away systems.

"Blood"

It is past midnight,
I'm not a vampire,
but I'm thirsty for
fresh blood.

I'm 20 years old,
in 20 years I will be
thirsty for tea
and in another 20 years,
it will be vegetable soup.

That's life!

"A scar on my face"

When this love left me,
it left a deep scar
on my face.

This scar is all I'll ever have,
from a brutal love.

In this playground
or Russian roulette,
sometimes you win,
sometimes you lose.

You might find love,
that lasts forever
and that leaves a smile
on your face.

Mine went away
and left a deep
scar on my face.

"Broken heart"

In the crude
and rude playground
of existence,
the heart,
at the early
stages of life,
is unbroken,
an unbreakable motor.

But then it comes
that time in which,
the mechanisms,
parameters
and physics
of your pumping core
system,
are completely
re-programmed.

The main aorta,
starts pumping venom,
the beat increases
and it feels like the
heart wants to explode
in fragments.

What the heart was before,
the heart is no more.

This is called a
broken heart.

"The equation and the parameters"

An equation is a mathematical tool
based on two sets of operations
connected by an equal sign.

An equation is the true
representation of everything
God has created.

Love is described by an equation.

In the love operations,
there are the two
infatuated individuals.

The equal sign is the
aorta vein of the relationship,
a communication channel
and the two parts,
on the opposite sides,
must play the game
of life and death
to balance the
mathematical statement.

What is added by the left
individual must be also
added by the right individual.

This also works for subtractions,
divisions
and multiplications.

If the two souls mismatch
parameters,
then the equation will fail
and in a cascade,
the bond between
the two as well.

This is the
life equation,
brutal,
honest
and not
for everyone.

"Dimidium"

Half the mass of Jupiter,
Dimidium is the next big mystery.

In the playground of science,
astronomers and cosmologists,
Dimidium has been found.

A new potential exoplanet,
a gas semi-giant,
in the constellation of
Pegasus, just 50 light years
away, a weekend trip.

473,036,538,855,978 Km away from us.

A distance that mankind cannot even imagine.

Sadly in our era
we will never get there physically,
but only with our imagination.

Nothing stops us from
imagining our spaceship
approaching Dimidium,
also called 51 Pegasi b.

I can see poor Dimidium,
all alone in the vacuum of space.

Orbiting a sun-like star,
all alone in a space so vast

and so remote,
where silence is king,
absence is king,
majestic views are king
and the orbiting which
will end within
a few billion years.

"Elysian fields"

If on this blue marble ball
you will encounter grace,
on Elysian fields
shall you be
in the afterlife,
when you will be no more,
but your soul will
whisper in eternity,
things never
heard before.

"My inner monologues"

I'm an introvert,
I might be great in
counseling,
but my day is pretty dark.

I'm full of colours
and huge stories within.

From within
I look like a
Chinese New Year's day.

I'm transparent,
almost a ghost,
but within I'm
writing the bible
take two.

"Into Elysium"

Have I earned
to walk onto
Elysian fields?

Where there
are no storms,
but only heroes,
with blue curly hair,
golden bows,
just posing there?

Have I earned
my right to eternity?
Where women can
finally, dance naked,
around a green fire?

I've earned it.

I've made it.

"No arms, no legs"

I ended up
on this hospital bed, why?

I ask God,
but all I hear
are the nurses chatting.

All I hear
is the sound of the machine
attached to my body.

Days seem endless
and in my mind I see love;
I see only a blurred image
of a thing called love.

Soon this image
will become transparent,
soon I will bee alone,
alone with my thoughts
and the hope
of euthanasia.

A sad story.

"The battle of us two"

You are Adolf,
I am Winston.

We fought back in 1940,
"on the landing grounds,
on the beaches,
we never,
ever surrendered."

Love is war
and love is the empty artillery shells.

Love is the shrapnel in my left leg.

Love is the Swastika on your arm.

You are the Bismarck,
I'm HMS Hood.

I'm going down,
with all of my resources
and you're going down too.

Our Admirals sent a last message,
honoring the fatherland
and saying "We will fight until the end."

Then Barbarossa,
you froze to death,
while the Red Army
strategy was to retreat,
to make you slowly die in the cold.

At the end we have both lost,
gained nothing
and left a trail
of anguish,
death
and sorrow.

We need humanitarian help.

"Just let it go"

Seat on a green meadow,
put both palms of your hands on the grass.

Let your 10 fingers
become roots,
let them penetrate
deep in the ground.

Now wait for the 1000 storms,
wait for the 1000 deaths,
wait for the 1000 knives
about to stab your chest.

She is gone
and these things
are about to happen.

Let the scorpions,
snake
and spiders bite you.

Don't worry,
these things
will not eradicate
your solid roots.

The roots will keep
you still and stable.

Just let this one go away.

"Balance"

I am not talking about accounting,
I am not interested in weighing scales.

Balance is the order of life,
it is the central
pillar of the entire Universe.

In balance with the seasons,
animals adapt.

In balance,
we grow older.

Loose balance and you lose your life.

Loose balance and you lose your head.

Wealth and health,
are based on balance.

I regret to say,
that while I was
walking on the narrow
path of life,
I fell into the void.

I fell into the 4th Dimension.

I came back and became
an observer,
not a doer.

You might spend
all your life balancing,
creating mountains of balancing
well positioned stones.

But once you fall
your castle crumbles
and you have to start all over,
from the bottom.

The good thing is that is never too late.

"In a cube"

Voluntarily
I entered the cube.

The cube has
glass walls
and once in it,
it locks forever
and it is suspended
high above.

"Oily surface"

Balance is King in life.

I'm always walking
on an oily surface.

Falling on the left,
right, back
and forward,
down,
but never upward.

I fall to the point
that I'm covered in oil.

But day by day
I fall less and less
and this makes me smile.

I'm learning
to stand still,
to walk firmly.

I'm learning
this impossible thing
called balance.

"Rats"

Rats have conquered
our beautiful marble ball.

They are everywhere,
in every hole
and breaks in walls.

Little eyes watch us,
study us, inspect us.

We are on the verge
of initiating a war,
humans against rats.

I'm sure rats will win,
for being the smallest,
the most resilient
and the smartest.

Once we humans
are out of the way,
rats will face an invasion
from cockroaches.

The real survivors of this story.

One day cockroaches
might succumb to ants,
ants to bacteria,
bacteria to protozoa.

"Post traumatic stress disorder"

The battlefield of life,
mortars
and bayonets.

The Generals release the order
and troops must advance.

I remember that moment when I
got out of the trench,
that moment when an
enemy bullet got
me on one leg,
millimeters away
from the great
saphenous vein.

It was so painful,
I felt no pain.

It was so sad,
I felt no sadness.

It was so dangerous,
I saw no danger.

That moment has become
the keeper of my life.

"Assonance and consonance"

Love.

The natural type of love
is us.

I'm the assonance,
you're the consonance.

Similar in sound,
but different in shape
and structure.

We walk hand in hand,
because we are
the puzzle of love in
which the two parts
of this whole,
have to attach to
each other with harmony.

Like tears with no fears,
like tex and mex
and like you and me,
we are the difference,
the difference in the
equality of love.

In this puzzle of love,
we are soul mates,
but I'm the assonance
and you are the consonance.

"The ocean liner and the rouge wave"

The rogue wave,
the seventh wave.

Is it an evil wave?
Is the wave you?
My lover tormenting
me day and night?
Why are you beating
me so hard?

I'm having a hard time
trying not to sink.

I'm the heavy and
unsinkable ocean
liner named "Dreamer"
and you are the rogue wave,
named "Collision."

"Shoes without laces"

When I was a kid,
there was no money
to buy me shoes.

I had a pair of
old leather shoes,
without laces
and much bigger
then my size.

It was difficult
to walk in them
and keep the balance.

I kept on falling.

In a way,
I am thankful,
because I have learned
the art of keeping the balance
in life, from an early age.

This balance is
the law of life.

"Binary System"

We are attracted
one to another.

My gravitational
pull is much
stronger than yours.

Yours is weaker,
but it affects
everything that
happens to me.

I orbit around an axis,
you circle around me.

I'm the alpha,
you are the omega.

For billions of years,
we'll form the Binary
System of love.

The Binary System
of us two.

"Early emotional neglect"

I'm a grown-up,
I should be fine,
I should be confident
and sane.

Instead this dark
cloud embraces me
and won't let go.

It's an invisible thing,
that I feel every single day.

Sometimes I manage
to have a sunny day,
most of the time the
storm inside roars like a lion.

Something must
be wrong with me,
I can't understand,
this state of mind I'm in.

I must be an alien,
a new species.

I do not belong among
the living, I feel numb,
empty.

I depend, I can't let go.

Whatever I do, is wrong,
cause I'm just incapable

of doing things.

I'm too hard on myself,
soft with others.

My vocabulary is limited,
I cannot express my feelings.

The subtle and the invisible spirit is upon me.

I need a way out,
I need to be re-born,
perhaps with different parents.

"Romance is for weak minds"

Flowers and
chocolate,
rhymes and
poems,
kisses and hugs,
for the weak
of the heart.

But rudeness and
shouting,
offending and tears,
is it any better?

So far we have come
and yet no progress
made on love.

Love is still a
fortress,
difficult to conquer.

Love is still
a parasite,
a virus,
that consumes
our lives.

"Oumamua"

As usual
opinions are mixed.

They are aliens,
they are not aliens.

I like to think
that the angels
have arrived.

They are just
protecting us.

I do not want
to think,
that they are
hostile beings.

That would be bad.

Due to our
primitive technologies,
we will never know.

"Speed of light"

I'm in a fast car
and I am not the driver.

The driver drives fast,
free as a bird,
without responsibility.

I get my note pad.

At over 100 Km per hour,
the world is different.

What would happen,
if we would surpass
the speed of light?

At this speed,
I am not able to distinguish
people's faces.

I see fast pillars of colours
and objects distorted by our speed.

All goes well until we suddenly crash.

A major frontal crash.

I can see
the crash from above,
I can see myself dying.

Suddenly a bright light above me.

A portal opens up.

I can fly toward the light,
at incredible speed,
reaching the center of this
bright sun
and becoming light myself.

"Will power"

I close my eyes
and I visualize
myself in the future.

I have won,
in the future
I won everything.

I became an augmented
human with powers,
not money,
because in the future
money will have no meaning.

Power will be calculated
based on your intelligence,
which will become
the new trading
currency.

As an augmented
superhuman,
I can fly and watch the
world from above.

Watch the ants, the workers.

This is where
I want to be,
there's nothing
that can stop me,
even if I kill
to get there.

There's nothing wrong
in being self-motivated,
but be aware that curiosity
killed the cat.

"That day"

The day will come,
in which the machines
will look at themselves
in a mirror and will
get emotional.

That day is so close,
that it is believed,
that this type
of super machines,
will be our very last
invention.

This is a natural process,
called selection,
not caused by nature
in this instance,
but caused by our curiosity
and caused by the fact,
that we want
to play being God.

That day will soon come
and procreation, as a process,
will change.

When the day will finally come,
money will lose
value and meaning,
food will have no sense,
love and hate will be things of the past.

It will be the way of the machines.

Only the so-called
super-intelligence
will survive
and life on heart
will become
unrecognizable.

"The next big thing"

The white and crisp future,
will be a place
where money is not needed.

In the future,
humans will be immortal
and our basic needs,
will change forever.

Jobs will be a thing of the past.

Men will have time to think and dream.

This is the leap,
the so-called augmented life,
in which we will be in control
even of our age.

This leap, will be our next
massive evolution jump,
in which our brain will be
the center of the universe.

The augmented brain,
half biological and half
synthetic will be a true
marvel of technology.

We will be the next big thing,
we as individuals will become
Gods, scientists, heroes.

We will become what

we want to become
and our slaves,
the machines,
will do the job for us.

Obviously this will happen
if our plans will work out.

There could always
be a machine revolt
against us.

If that happens,
machines will become
the next big thing.

"The post-humans world"

Soon super-intelligence,
will rise so high,
that we, the ants,
will not even be
able to understand it.

As the ants have been
crushed by the concrete,
we will be broken
in many different ways.

We are surrounded by it
already.

It is already too late.

Faith has been already
written and executed,
faster by the day.

The only vision I have,
is myself in a beautiful field,
laying on the grass,
under the sun.

All of this will go,
it's a fact.

"Standard acceleration of free fall"

According to
the laws of nature
and God,
the closer you
get to me,
the faster you
will get to me.

As a matter of fact,
our attractions,
has got even more
intense as you get
closer and closer to me.

You are on the
other side
of the world,
very far away
from me.

So why is gravity working?

This gravitational
field that surrounds me
and you is not other
than something called love.

"Masks"

A person that
has suffered from
early childhood neglect,
will be wearing masks
through his or her entire life.

Different masks,
according to the intensity
of the trauma.

I've been wearing
Noh masks since
I was born.

My life is a masked
drama-dance performance
and just like a mystical
Noh play,
I'm the Mae-shite,
then the Nochi-shite.

It's a bizarre life wearing
masks.

I have many masks.

Sometimes I'm a Kagekiyo,
then I'm a Kumasaka,
other times I'm Yase-onna,
then again a Kishin
or a Shishiguchi.

I will complete the cycle
of this bizarre Noh play,
wearing a Okina mask,
the old man.

"Small details"

Life is a scale,
life is a line
and from the moment
you are born,
it has been narrated,
like a tale
and it has been
well organized
into chapters,
just like a book.

I believe in simplicity,
in living a simple
and noble life,
but it is true
that a life with less details,
is a life with less honor.

It is up to you,
how much details
you put into your life.

I rather live a life
full of details,
because once the lady
in black comes,
your life will be measured
and your role,
in the afterlife
will be given
according to the
level of your details.

The greatest
the details,
the more
likely will be,
that you will be
transferred to Elysium.

"You cannot escape a catastrophe"

A beautiful day out,
not summer,
not spring.

The 7th wind
caresses my skin.

I close my eyes and
thoughts of an aseptic,
immense future
run through my head.

The future
is embedded
in the fabric of me.

I embrace it.

I'm hopeful,
I'm happy,
I feel immortal.

We live our life
with a sense
of immortality;

we are confident,
that we'll be
around when the
sun will die.

There are many

projects and plans
in my head.

I'm busy, wealthy
and healthy.

In this glorious day,
I cross an empty road.

I do not look on
my right
and suddenly
I can fly.

I'm flying.

A brute force
has pushed me in
the air, on a journey
never taken before.

On a journey through
the clouds of the Gods.

I can see myself
on the side of the road.

I am not moving.

The roads are
painted blood red.

All of the sudden
between me
and reality,

there is a wall
made of thick glass.

I bang on this wall,
I cry, I call people
on the other side.

They cannot see me,
nor they can hear me.

They never will.

"Vicious circularity"

Our love is more then just love,
our love is a vicious circle,
made of complex things,
mental illness
and paradoxes.

The circularity
goes in this way,
I love you because
I was born to love you
and the same is for you.

After two days I hate you
and you hate me too.

We split up,
because we want to,
then we both cry.

We cannot stay together,
we cannot live apart,
so we love each other again.

We have a disease called
"Vicious Circularity of Love Syndrome,"
in which everything goes
around and around,
ad infinitum.

"Hymn to Kursk"

Atomnaya Podvodnaya Lodka "Kursk,"
this is a hymn to you
and for the 118
Poseidon kids,
returned to their
lives in the abyss
and lost in the immense blue.

The Barents Sea,
is now your grave
and you are the witnesses of
the stupidity of war
and the madness of man,
at the highest of the levels.

While at the bottom
and still alive,
for six intense hours,
the 118 were in
God's hands.

Suddenly that precious
thing called oxygen,
was no more
and the 118 passed
to a better world.

"The introverted Aries"

Within the
continuum space
of time, there's
the "Introverted
Aries Paradox."

I feel like I'm
one of a kind.

I'm a roaring
Aries and
a shy introverted
individual.

At night I'm
a werewolf,
hungry for blood;

during the day
I'm an angel,
shy and locked
in my world.

Even though
I feel like the ship
of Theseus,
I will always live
a life of contradictions,
interrelated differences,
conspiracies
and controversies.

"Female spirits of sea waters"

Poseidon did well
as a father,
but one of his
nymphs will
no longer carry
his trident.

She'll be my
lover day
and night.

I've fallen
in love with
Galatea
and when
I'll die, she will
make me into
an eternal spirit.

She's got the
powers to do so.

"Andromeda and Perseus"

Cetus,
with its dark claws,
embraces you,
without knowing,
that it's head
will be cut off,
with the sharpest blade,
the fiery sword
of the 8th heaven.

Shortly my love,
you will become
with me, one soul,
one and only one Jewel.

We are a jewel
and there
will be no more chains,
around you,
no high tide,
no abnormal wave
to interfere with us.

You are my Andromeda.

I'm reaching out to you.

I will save you,
from the monsters
of society.

"Why do people cheat?"

I've never broken
the rules,
I've never won
out of dishonesty,
I'm not a fraud,
I'm a good man,
heading to Elysium,
hopefully.

Society is a Tsunami.

In a Tsunami,
there is everything:
dark and white things.

The darkness prevails
in men's heart
therefore by cheating
men will make millions.

I hope that one day,
the sooner the better,
evolution will lead
us to the next step
of society,
an aseptic
and translucent culture,
where brains are
programmed differently.

"The Spirits of Order"

I must climb K2,
I must reach the peak.

Once I achieve this,
I will open my arms,
I will accept the spirits of order
into my body.

These spirits
will teach me
to make sense of
the chaos that now
resides in my weak heart.

Once they enter my body,
the second part of the ritual
will start.

I will have to jump
into the void of reality.

The free fall is needed,
to meet the spirits of
comprehension.

Once in me,
I will pull the line
and shoot the parachute.

Descending through the clouds
and wind, will allow me to meditate
and contemplate my existence.

While up there,
if a hawk will guide me,
then my task will be completed.

Touch down,
I feel the grass on my hands.

I'm on my knees
accepting the spirits,
all of them into me.

They are in me,
I feel wiser
and glorious.

I am now able
to face life
and meet you.

I just became
a free spirit of the land,
fire and water.

"Things have happened for a reason"

Divine intervention is real,
God is the player,
we are the actors of this
playground made
of immortal
and mortal things.

If we met at a crossroad,
or if we suddenly die,
we go through
well planned
and orchestrated
series of events.

Nothing is random
and everything
belongs to the whole.

Just like a very
weird painting
or an ancient
and colourful mosaic.

We do not understand this,
because we are mortals
and do not have the powers
to influence all living
and non-living things.

Things happen for a reason,
just like the clouds
became part of the mountains.

Just like the
river flows into
the valley
and just like a bird
belongs to the skies.

It has all been planned.

"100 km"

War, greed, tears, despair.

Nothing compares,
to the 100 km
atmosphere,
of our blue marble ball.

I see stealing,
killing,
tragedies,
catastrophes
and I wonder,
if only a man could
understand,
our unstable
position in
the Cosmo.

A slight change
in planetary physics
and we become history.

If only man
could understand,
that at only 100 km
above our heads,
there is nothing,
there is no oxygen,
there's no place to run to
and it's cold
and quiet up there.

These scary thoughts
should be enough,
to embrace love,
goodness
and altruism.

Remember that
at altitude 101 km,
we become children
of the stars.

"A dream"

Last night, I had two
occurrences of sleep paralysis
and many interrupted dreams.

Why so many dreams?
Why so many dreams about faith?
Are these prophecies?
Am I an Oracle? Can I read
or create the future?

Has society evolves,
dreams are becoming scary.

Visions of the Apocalypse,
fill my mind.

Visions of the future
do not go away.

I can see the future,
I have seen and been
in the new era,
I have seen the augmented reality
and it is scary.

"The best of me"

I always want to
give you the best,
but I'm still a beast.

Must be my mental disorder.

I'm incapable
of generating
goodness.

I can only supply
you with a good
dosage of emptiness.

This emptiness is a cry for help.

"Violence"

The so-called ultra-violence,
is embedded in the fabric
of this society.

Violence is a lady,
a beautiful lady,
worshiped
by millions.

Why is it that
violence becomes dopamine?
Why is it that men
long for blood?

Why does the nature
of society has to be built
on conquering countries?

Why everything has to be so
intoxicated?

The answer
is in men's heart.

The heart
has been violated
a long time ago
and since then,
it has never recovered from evil.

"Bad with words"

I am an introverted,
I am not good with words.

To me words represent
1000 knives, sharp ones.

I prefer telepathy,
I prefer to look into your eyes.

Thoughts are honey,
they are freedom.

Words complicate everything.

Words can hurt.

In a world made
of words, information,
debates, politics
and discussions,
I choose this candle,
the darkness of my room
and the sound of
the lonely wind outside.

"A story"

Once upon a time,
I went into the
deep, dark and
far away woods.

There step by step,
I got rid of all of
my belongings.

I got rid of my wallet,
I got rid of my smart jacket.

I let my hair grow,
I let my beard grow
and was wearing
an animal skin
to keep me warm.

After 6 months,
my body became stronger
and all my senses improved.

I finally got rid of
the pills and the morphine.

I built a refuge
and hunting tools.

I became primitive again,
like our ancestors 10,000 years ago.

I left beyond society,
I do not remember
my age any more,
I do not remember
my name any more.

I am nature,
I am the trees,
I am the insects
and all the animals
of the forest.

I am the hawk,
flying high in the sky,
through valleys
and high peaks.

I am all of this.

"The 4th industrial revolution"

The future of humanity,
is in your hands.

The brand new fabric
of a new augmented life,
is being built,
at this very moment,
in labs.

Today we are humans plus
and tomorrow we'll be
humans plus, plus.

In this revolution,
there is no difference
between true and false,
one and zero,
on and off.

The cube
or sphere,
embraces all of us
and we become immortals.

We live even if we die.

Images of things,
that you can touch only
by wearing special glasses,
are the cocaine and heroin
of this era.

Our life has become a touch
screen, made of colourful shapes,
that exists in augmented reality.

It makes me wonder if I exist,
or if I am only a fantasy, a program.

I ask my self if biology is real
or if my trillion cells
are only synthetic dots.

The industrial
revolution of today,
has nothing to do
with steam power,
but it deals with
the next level of
intelligence,
in which even
though the human
brain is shrinking in size,
it will always be connected,
to a higher entity
and it will be augmented
using special interfaces.

"Sand"

It's a hot day,
I'm on this endless beach.

I seat down for a moment,
no shoes, my feet in the sand.

I feel the heat of this beautiful
white sand.

Sand is like life.

Sand can devour you
and penetrate everywhere,
under your finger nails,
in your eyes,
in your hears
even in your sandwich.

There is a lesson
to be learned here.

You cannot get rid of sand,
but you can get rid of
the grains in your heart,
the grains in your veins
so that your existence
is clean and flows
without obstacles.

"Life and death"

Life is like death,
like brother and sister
linked in eternity.

The struggle of life
results in death, the pain,
the suffering, they joy,
positive and negative
poles are all linked
in this playground
of life and death.

Do not despair,
don't let the anguish get to you.

Enjoy, relax, be happy,
because we do not know
when the Harvester
will come for us.

So do not think
about money,
do not think
about possessions
and do not think
about stability.

The only stable
and real thing
is the day you are born
and the day you will die.

"My uncontrollable anger toward you"

It is difficult to understand,
why I am so abusive toward you.

The police have come a few times.

We are at a point in which
next time they will arrest us.

We are at a breaking point.

I'm an angry man,
under a pale gray sky.

You are a joyful girl,
under a dark blue sky,
full of fluffy clouds.

This is how it was
and how it's going to be.

They are knocking on the door.

It's the police.

"Funeral"

A few days ago,
my best friend died,
in a horrible accident.

Today we are all
gathered at the
town cemetery,
for his funeral.

The whole town
showed up,
he was a popular guy.

Wait a minute,
the guy in the casket
it's me.

I'm dead,
I'm energy.

Need to fly away,
I need to fly away.

"For her"

This body is for her,
this money,
all of it,
is for her.

These possessions,
are for her,
my heart and
my soul are for her.

Nothing else
I can do,
she is keeping me
as a hostage.

"No more love"

Life has given me,
a solid mind,
a bunch of dreams
and a disabled body.

Sometimes life
has given me love,
now and then.

Love has taught me
the rules of everything,
but at this stage in my life,
I say no to more love,
because I do not
want to lose
my sanity.

"The fog"

Ice crystals
and water droplets,
create fog.

You are in suspended
animation.

You come
from the sky
perhaps, or
who knows
from where.

Are you different
from the mist?
Do you hide things?
Do you hide monsters?
Tonight you came.

Visibility was 0%
and you were white,
fluffy, thick and heavy.

Tonight I made up my
mind, I will run to you,
I will hide in you.

Lift up my body,
take me to places.

"Metamorphosis"

This is not the novel
by Kafka,
it's a story
about change.

I have changed,
I was a caterpillar
and now I'm a butterfly,
or a moth because
I love the dark
of the night.

I am perfection,
I love to fly free
in the open sky
and in every direction.

I do not like chains
and I do not like to be
told off.

I do love my freedom.

"Soldiers"

I belong to this
band of brothers.

Together we
advance through
enemy lines,
together we stand
and together we fall.

We are like one machine,
with guns and we are
hungry for more blood.

If one of us dies,
we suffer and usually
have our revenge.

We think as one,
like ants.

But all of the sudden,
I think I'm a murderer
and sometimes
I have enjoyed it.

This must be wrong.

"Hymn to a mother"

Dear Mother,
I know you are
so far away
from me.

I know I
haven't spoken
to you as I
should have.

I know that
you have never
told me that
you loved me,
because you
are introverted.

Despite this,
you are at
the centre
of my heart.

When I'll die,
your name
will appear
like a tattoo,
right on my chest.

"Please don't hate me"

Anger
or resentment,
strong emotions,
are ready to explode,
in each one of us.

If you do have
to hate me,
make sure this
hate is short-lived
and not long-lasting.

Hatred is ignorance,
in the sense that,
you hate me
if you don't know me.

You should
get to know me,
I might be a box of
precious stones
and gems,
you never know.

Understand that
extreme hate,
can be a crime,
therefore put away
your frustrations,
hate crime,
hate speech,
be wise,
be smart,

be sharp
and kind.

I beg you please,
do not hate me.

"Sad love"

Love supposed to be
as tall as a skyscraper,
robust as the 7
pillars of the world,
deep as the
deepest ocean
and strong as the
strongest wind.

Instead
this love is
weak as a wet paper,
breakable as thin ice,
melting as butter in
a frying pan
and broken
as a broken heart.

"Sensei"

Look beyond,
look ahead.

When you reach
the horizon,
find another wider
and brighter
horizon.

When you reach
the bottom of a
deep ocean,
seek for more
and never stop.

Conquer another mile
and another one
and another one.

Do not worry about
reaching the end
because there is no end.

The earth is a sphere,
march on it,
experience it.

You'll become a Sempai,
then a Sensei,
then Dai-Sensei
and you will
reach the heavens.

"Child abuse"

Please don't touch me,
I don't belong to you,
I'm not an object,
I'm just a child,
scarred for life,
because of you,
because of your
bad drunk breath
and your rough hands.

I will never,
ever forget you
and you will hear
from me in the future.

The wrath of God
will be upon you.

"Our divorce"

We used to be one.

There was no
separation between us
and every situation,
was supposed to be
forever and ever.

We came to this anomaly
in our life.

This anomaly has the sound of a cello.

A very deep and dark sound.

We used to be
two inseparable Orcas.

Orcas stay together for life
while humans don't.

It must be because
Orcas have a bigger
brain than ours.

You need brains
to stay together,
to be able to control
emotions which
can destroy the balance
and not guts.

"The fire inside me"

I just woke up,
it's 5am,
so early.

I wake up with the
rooster and chickens
and I am ready to go.

I'm the rooster,
the Gallus Gallus Domesticus.

I'm the man,
with fire in my heart.

I'm the rooster,
guarding the weak under me.

I do the Cocketer "waltz"
and conquest females.

I engage in cock-fighting
at work.

Just as the rooster can't sleep,
I can't sleep neither,
because I am a dreamer,
with fire in my hands,
eyes
and heart.

"Your words are knives"

You remind me
of Polyphemus,
the Cyclop from
Homer's Odyssey.

I am Ulysses,
escaping from you
on my ship.

I blinded you,
therefore you are
in an uncontrollable
rage.

You are so enraged
that saliva comes
out of your mouth.

There is no more
air in your
lungs at times.

Your words are
as sharp as knives.

I'm on my ship,
you are about to
throw at me
a huge rock,
but I escape
unarmed.

You are blinded

for life
because you
only had one eye.

Your father
Poseidon
and your
mother Thoosa,
are not proud of you.

"Good morning, good bye"

It's 6am,
I wake up
before you.

I try not to
wake you up.

I leave the room,
I get ready quietly,
I must not wake you up.

I manage to put
a few things
in my backpack.

I even pack up
some food.

Finally,
I open the door
and get out
of the house,
I am about to open
the car's door.

I forget the keys.

I get back into
the house,
thank God I
did not lock the
main door.

All quiet
and you are still
sleeping.

All of a sudden,
you are in front of me
and you say to me:
Are you looking for this?

"Dogfight"

A Spitfire
and a Messerschmidt.

1940, over the
skies of Kent.

My house is
120 years old.

My house
has witnessed
the bombings
and dogfights.

What a privilege to be here.

I just touch these
ancient bricks
and I'm connected
immediately.

I can hear the
sounds of engines
of the super-marines.

I can hear the sound
of machine guns
and explosions.

I can see blood flowing
down the streets.

What a tragedy war is.

"The box of precious stones"

I have a bunch
of tiny stones
in my hand.

I lift my hand.

I let the stones fall.

One by one the stones
fall down and form a pile.

The pile gets taller and taller.

Some stones are dark,
some others are white.

They are all mixed.

You never take
stones out of
your pile;

you sum
precious gems
to your collection
every single day.

Life is a pile of precious
and untouchable stones.

"More fine sand"

Grains of fine sand
are all over me,
it seems like
they want to push me
into the hole.

While I lay on
this beautiful beach,
the sand covers me
brought in by the wind.

If I don't move,
the send will
slowly cover me.

This reminds me of life.

If you are constantly in a
comfortable position,
you will get to a
point when you
won't be able
to escape the sand.

You have to fight
the sand,
you have
to move and climb
out of the hole.

"Best day of my life"

Today I feel
the souls of
the ancient ones
getting into my
flesh and bones.

Today it's a fresh day,
today I'm not
concerned
any more
about the
dark side.

The book of life
is finally opened
on a good chapter.

I don't want to
rush through
this ancient book.

I just want to read
one page per day,
learn as much as I can
and breath the smell
of the book
because it's the
best fragrance.

"Another dream"

I had another dream,
one in which you fall,
in an endless fall,
in a dark abyss.

In this dream
I was falling
and spiraling
out of control.

I woke up.

I'm still falling.

"My heart doesn't bit any more"

How awful is the
process of growing up.

I look like an older man,
I have gray hair,
I have scars all over
my body.

But I'm a kid at heart.

I no longer run,
I no longer jump,
I no longer reach the skies
and my heart does
not beat any-more.

"Orion and the great pyramid of Giza"

Beta Orions
and Alpha
Orion are
never alone,
they are always
with their father,
the Constellation
of Orion.

They shine in
the night sky.

They are colourful
and together,
form Orion's belt.

The Gigantic Hunter,
has something to do
with the Great Pyramid of Giza
and science doesn't
know why.

"Adultery"

I admit that
I have committed
adultery.

By having done so,
I have deprived my wife,
of lost opportunities
that will never come back.

Adultery is
like the disease
of jealousy,
it affects the
whole harmony
and dynamics
of love.

At the end,
the man or woman,
who commits the
crime of adultery,
will carry within
their heart,
their own
prison sentence.

"Genetics"

The struggle of
the fittest,
is a thing of the
past.

Today's men,
will soon be
replaced by
the perfect men,
engineered in labs.

Perfect,
with a clean,
disease-free
and pristine DNA.

At the end
evolution has
been compromised.

There has been
a breach in the
natural system of
things and ecology,
caused by
the plastic man.

"2000 years old tree"

I have walked miles and miles,
in this ancient forest,
just to come and see you.

Now I stand right in front of you.

You are 2000 years old today
and I came to wish
you a happy birthday.

I also came to ask you,
to make me wise and special,
special as you are.

You have seen history,
you have witnessed men stupidity,
in all these centuries
and in all its glory.

Please pass me
your knowledge,
your kindness
and your fountain
of eternal youth.

"Pareidolia in love"

Sometimes you think
that love is smooth, steady
and solid.

But love is tricky,
love is devilish.

Love makes you
believe things
that actually
do not exist.

Love has its own mind,
its own intelligence
and special powers.

Love can make
you see illusions
and rob you
of your life.

Love is cruel,
it's the rule
of the jungle.

"Where is Babylon?"

They tell me to go north,
then they say go west.

There is
no need to move,
to migrate,
like an exotic bird does.

I carry my Babylon
within myself.

No need to be wealthy
because my wealth
is my dignity.

I am the owner
of my own special
Babylon,
which is even
richer then
Shangri-La.

"We don't click"

My dear love,
we do not click.

Clicking means,
being compatible.

Clicking means,
being able
to talk without
saying a word.

I see nothing
too special,
I see no bond,
I see no conspiracy,
I see no future.

How sad to let you go,
but whatever you do
and wherever you may go,
I will send you my
blessing,
always.

"Hymn to my father"

My dear father,
you are a
beautiful spirit
in this whole world.

All I can do,
with great honor,
is to sing to you
and to write rhymes
about you.

You left me
many years ago
and since then,
you have been
watching me,
from the seventh sky,
dressed up
as a penguin,
elegant,
with class,
you give me direction
and your name
is tattooed on
my soul.

Father, you are a
beautiful spirit
in this world.

"Fibromyalgia"

Welcome Fibro,
I love you Fibro,
you are mine,
you are here to stay.

I might be a masochist,
and enjoy the 24/7
pain you give me.

What would I do,
or be without you?

With you,
I'm the king
of the disabled.

People point fingers
at me because of you
and I feel kind of special.

You are attached to me,
in an eternal, hot
and cold embrace.

With you,
I can go to places,
I can think and meditate.

I became a
better person,
because of you.

While thanks to you,
I have the time to
write my thoughts,
others are forever
entangled to a 9 to 5
torture.

I love you Fibro.

"Borderline"

The Borderline
mental disorder,
reminds me of two
of Picasso's famous paintings:
"Dora maar au chat"
and "Girl before a mirror."

While these
paintings might
depict love or just
portraits,
their colours,
intensity, surrealism
and madness,
can also describe
the craziness of
being borderline.

The excess of bright
colours and dark colours,
depicting highs and lows,
the straight lines representing
the edge, are the parameters
of a formula that
drives you mad
and the shapes,
make you stand
on the razor's edge.

"The love equation 2"

The love equation result,
is equal to all the
things contained
in this world,
minus two equal parts,
myself and you.

"If love is you"

If love is death,
then I will run away from it.

If love is a star in the sky,
I will look at it over and over again.

If love is a flower,
I will water it every day.

But if love is you
and only you,
then I will fall in love
with you
and only you.

"Storm of war"
Life is a storm of war
and we are in the middle
of this battlefield,
playing the game
of life and death.

"Rain"
Rain always start at the wrong time and the wrong
place and when it starts, I never have an umbrella with
me.

"Late"
I am late with everything, but I will be ok.

"A ripple in the fabric of space-time"

I was told that I was
conceived and
born by mistake.

I was told that
I was an extra,
a baby surplus,
something not
needed and
not even loved.

As a matter of fact, no-one
has ever told me "I love you."

The pain in my heart is immense
and this life seems like a torture,
every day, every hour, minute
and second.

But I will make it big.

I will fly as a bird, high
above the clouds of Mars
and Venus.

I will make a difference.

I am a ripple,
in the fabric
of space and time.

"Thermonuclear warfare"

Nothing learned
from "Little Boy"
and "Fat Man."

How scary are the words
Nuclear Reactor,
Fallout,
Nuclear winter
and Uranium.

How scary is the Roar of
a Nuclear Explosion,
in a place near you.

How scary is the mind of the
wrong global leader,
at the wrong time
and at the wrong place,
pushing the wrong
red old button.

It doesn't matter if
it is a limited,
or a full-scale
nuclear war.

Man will never learn
and man will end it all.

At the end,
the beauty that man
has created,

will be destroyed
by man's hands.

A creation, without its creator.

"Silly war games"

Before you kill
20 million people
before you push
those buttons,
turn those keys
and insert those
weird codes,
I would like
to say to you,
just right before launch,
few heavenly comments.

These silly war games,
will end our life,
they will end
the human-made heaven,
to start the human-made hell.

The so-called,
patriotic "Missileers,"
are capable of such
actions, because they
are locked in bunkers,
blind, trained and deaf.

They do love,
the human-made inferno.

"A false sense of security"

We are all so secure here on earth.

The extinction of dinosaurs,
is only a legend,
typically said to kids.

We are so secure on
our beautiful blue planet.

Climate change
is only a myth,
something that
will never touch
our lives.

So let's walk on these streets,
let's not think about what is
inevitable and imminent.

Let's not think about
Artificial Intelligence
taking over by force.

Humans are being attacked
and face extinction in
about 100 years.

This is a wake-up call,
to understand
that we are just ants.

"Desertification of the soul"

With great joy,
I say that the process
of desertification
of men's heart
has begun.

It will take
the entire
planet effort
to reverse
this process.

Men have become sad,
depressed, isolated.

Quality of life
is non-existent,
war all around
the globe
are spreading
like a virus.

The only thing
that can save us,
is planting trees,
million of them,
in every corner
of our souls
and heart.

"My pain"

Sometimes I think that
I dream too much.

Sometimes I wish I could
be drugged for eternity.

I could finally
lose myself
in Elysian gardens,
with blue hair
and naked.

I dream of running,
I dream of flying
and holding a
fluffy could
in my arms.

But I think that
I dream too much.

I think that
dreaming of being
able to transcend
this condition
of mine is
too good
to be true.

Transcend and overcome
the crucifixion of everyday pain.

How I wish dreams were a reality
and reality to be dreams.

I want to transcend,
please let me.

Let me transcend with love,
hope, harmony, grace,
humanity
and humility.

Let me overcome the pain.

My pain.

"Karman line"

If you look up,
all the way
up to the sky,
up until you
reach 100 km,
you will find
a delimiter.

This line defines
life and death,
on our beautiful
blue planet.

Right after that line,
is the incognito
of everything.

The unknown
of what's known
and the observable space
begins.

"2050"

I'm always dreaming
about the year 2050.

Will I be around?

If not, at least I will be
there as a ghost.

By that year, jobs might
be a thing of the past.

Everything might become
a human right, and for free,
because the machines will
work for us.

Will humans start fading away?
The rate of technological advancement
is so fast, that in 30 years,
scary things might happen.

This radical change, will
be inevitable.

The futuristic future will finally,
arrive and the new humans will
be different from us.

I can only imagine what
it's going to be like
and dream about it.

"Death of a King"

You were a young,
too young, clever
and beautiful King.

King of Jerusalem,
King of the crusaders,
King of Christianity
and of those cold nights
in the desert.

I heard you were good,
with the good ones and bad,
with the wicked ones.

You had a terrible disease
since you were young,
too young.

You died right before the fall of
Jerusalem.

Every time I listen to "Vide Cor Meum"
I cry non-stop.

Even though 1000 years separate us,
I feel you, I feel your disease
and strength of a great King.

You are my King,
King Baldwin.

"Home"

100 years
and our home
might die.

100 years
and we might
end up in the
mouth of a
black hole.

100 years away,
from a Planetary
catastrophe.

An extinction event.

Home is on a ring of the Milky Way.

I would not want to live anywhere else.

However, the world is dying.

Humanity is vanishing.

Hunger, wars, wickedness, tears,
are tragedies of everyday.

Let's change all of this.

Let's do it.

"A photon in a sea of energy"

I am traveling
at the speed of light.

I am floating away,
in a sea of light.

Through light
one can see time,
in the vast immensity of space.

Therefore, through me,
one can travel in time and space.

On the electromagnetic spectrum,
in the visible part, I'm an actor,
a very tiny dot in this immensity
created by God.

I only need energy to survive.

I love traveling
on the tails of gamma rays.

I have now reached the speed of light.

I have now reached earth,
the beautiful blue marble planet.

I am going to hit it hard!
Catch me if you can!

"The Albatross"

You are
the most legendary
of all birds.

Your flight
has a sound,
the sound
of Chopin
Nocturne No 20.

You fly in scary winds.

You come down,
gently
and gliding.

Observing
everything,
with your
curious eyes.

"The legend of
the Albatross,"
will be the title
of my new book.

"Habitable zone"

Around my body exists
a space made of magic.

This space is my special place,
the habitable zone,
built for you.

Only you have rights
in this space around my self.

Only you have a voice
in this magic aura.

The habitable zone is a zone
in which we kiss, the region
in which we touch and play.

In this zone you can build
your stable home.

I'm your home,
your guide,
I'm your oxygen,
your day
and night.

My role is to protect you from
comets, asteroids.

My job is to give you shelter,
from solar rays,
solar flares.

I'm your habitable zone,
your atmosphere
and around us
there are strong
magnetic fields.

"My own planetary system"

Father, you are the Sun,
playing with nuclear fusion.

Mother, you are the Gas Giant,
with your immense hurricanes.

We kids are
the Planetesimals,
busy with our
planet formation
and learning.

We are all gravitationally
bound.

We all live in a circular
motion around Daddy.

Mother, you protect us from
dangers like asteroids and comets.

Daddy you give us life.

We, Planetesimals,
grow and grow
until we complete
our life cycle.

Then we die,
we become sterile.

At the end,
we all die,

and become
dust that travels
at the speed of light.

We become dead particles,
in the immense plains
of the silent Universe.

"If I was a hawk"

If I was a hawk,
I would jump off
the highest peak.

I would get down
the valley very quickly.

If I was a hawk,
I would catch preys
in stealth mode,
I would be invisible.

If I was a hawk,
I would try to reach
the end of earth's
atmosphere,
just because I can.

And if I was a hawk,
I would just fly away,
in a place so remote,
that it would be
just me
and the tricks
I do up in
the blue sky.

"The Ring Tattoo"

I am a free man,
I am a sad man,
I am a confused man.

All I have left is a ring tattoo.

I was told that the intensity of
the tattoo is based on how often
the ring was used.

All I have left is this pale
line on my finger.

All that she has left is
the pale line on her finger.

The line is infinite,
the track is cruel.

The line reminds me
of all my failures,
of all my victories.

For her, it is pretty much the same.

Life events are lines,
lines on fingers.

Lines that remind us of who we were,
of who we are and where we
are going.

"The legend of gravitational pulls"

Gravity is a theory,
a well known and
approved approach.

It's the theory of you,
pulling me toward yourself.

Your pull is really intense,
so intense that not even light can escape.

I am in this immense pull.

I am locked in.

I am not able to escape your pull.

I will never be able to do so.

"The infinite future"

I am now standing on this mountain.

I am the observer of life.

The observer of
everything that is
in motion.

The wind pushes forward.

The wind is an essential
part of the infinite future.

The sky is red,
the Sun is low.

The wind roars
just like a lion.

I am alone,
in this reality,
in this infinite future.

There is no beginning,
there is no end,
there is only me,
surrounded by light
and thin air.

"Trans-humanism"

The day has come.

The date is irrelevant
because we are
so far in the future,
so far that men has
evolved into "The Thing."

Prosthetic limbs, fake lips,
fake skin and AI.

In this new augmented life,
I can be whatever I want.

My brain has been
uploaded into a thing.

This thing, can be anything.

I can move around
into this new space-time
reality called "The Sphere."

Yesterday I was a
synthetic nanobot,
today I'm free as a dolphin,
in an ocean without depths.

Classic evolution has stopped.

The augmented and synthetic
life has begun.

"Love the plague"

This love is
a plague,
more precisely
the bubonic plague.

This love is a rat,
that transmits
diseases.

The Black Death
has come back,
with this love
written in
black ink.

"If Love becomes extreme"

In love,
you can't be
yourself.

In love,
you must act.

In love,
you must react.

Why?

Love should be
spontaneous.

Love should be
hilarious.

If love
becomes extreme,
than this love
should not be
allowed to breath.

"Rotten flower"

I had a dream
about a rotting
flower.

I could see the flower,
dying in slow motion.

Dying a bit more
and a bit more,
in each scene of
the movie.

Along with the slow
death of this flower,
my heart also died.

This rose
was the last
one I gave you,
the one
you rejected.

"Love the beast"

Love,
again,
is a wild
mushroom,
a wild and
awesome
beast.

A beast
you will never
be able to tame.

A beast from
which you will
never be safe,
because of
its psychotic ways.

Love is the ultimate
beast, the ultimate
hunter.

Love is here now,
I am the chosen one,
I am the one
for the ritual.

Love is also
black, red
and white magic.

"Duality"

Duality means
two things
and not three.

Duality is
what you
show me
all the time.

Living with
you is like
being on
Mount Everest
one day
and at the bottom
of the ocean,
the following day.

Duality means,
a smile from you.

Duality also means,
you being mad at me
for no reason.

I do not like
your duality,
I long for
unity.

"I close my eyes"

I close my eyes,
it feels so good.

My eyes resting,
resting from
the awful reality
of every-day.

I close my eyes,
because I choose
to dream.

I choose not to
face reality.

What's reality
anyway?

So much better,
to close my eyes
and imagine to be
on Mars, on the Moon,
or on Mont Blanc.

I close my eyes,
you should try it
too.

"The art of arguing"

What's in an argument?

Why do we argue?

There is actually
no reason at all
to argue.

Imagine what we
could do with all
the time wasted
on arguing?

With all this time
available,
we could build
a magic castle.

We could build
Noah's Ark.

So what are we
arguing about?

"Almost gone"

Soon I will be gone.

Being here physically,
will be only an
untouchable
memory,
made of foam.

Now is now
and tomorrow,
will be tomorrow.

A special niche
of time and space,
in which physically
I will exist no more.

The sound of my voice,
will be heard no more,
the touch of my hands,
will be felt no more
and the look of my eyes,
will be directed elsewhere.

"A long trip"

I am about
to start a
long trip.

A trip to
the edge
of the
Universe.

It is a trip
to go far,
far and
away from
this horrible
place.

I'm alone
and convinced
and no one
will stop me.

"Abraham Lincoln"

This immense tale,
starts on the
12th of February 1809,
when a boy was born.

This boy,
did not want to be
like his father,
who was an
anti-intellectual.

Abraham,
grew up as
an honest man.

He became a well
respected lawyer.

Not bad as a
self educated politician
and congressman.

He wanted
to do good,
he believed in the
"American Dream."

The storm of war,
was against him,
a civil war,
never seen before
and while
the North

and the
South kept
on arguing,
he lead people
to believe
and to patriotism.

He preserved
the Union,
the Flag,
abolished slavery,
what a good
guy he was.

But make no
mistake,
the good boy,
was also a
mastermind,
a strategist,
a manipulator who
conquered the
White House
and built America.

Sadly he was
assassinated in
April 15, 1865,
just like all
the other public
figures in history.

"John F. Kennedy"

John is a common name,
but this man wasn't a
common man.

Number 35,
in the world
most important list,
this man was responsible
to bring back home
moon dust,
"not because it was
easy, but because it
was hard."

The so called,
space race with
the Russians,
culminated in Apollo,
son of Zeus, going
around sister Moon,
11 times,
then touching ground,
where there was,
and there's only
"beautiful desolation."

Down in Cuba,
with old Fidel,
the Big three,
almost started,
when war was cold,
you could not speak Russian
and missiles where

brought closer and
closer to the big
bold eagle.

You put your
hands and nose,
into too many things
and in Dallas,
at 12:30pm,
November 22, 1963,
you were sent,
very unfortunately,
to better life.

We all miss you
Mr. President.

"Martin Luther King"

You had a dream,
a dream of equality,
empathy and goodness,
in the far 1963.

You had a dream,
in which all men,
black and white,
could stand together,
in a common struggle.

Together,
in an alliance,
in a brotherhood.

Mr. King,
you were
and are,
probably,
the most famous
activist that ever lived
and you gave your
soul and mind,
for the principles
you preached to
millions.

This horrible thing
called, racial inequality,
today is called,
racial equality
thanks to you,
thanks to the storm

in your heart,
thanks to your speeches.

The communist ties
and other bad
conspiracies against you,
did not help though
and during the
occupation of D.C.,
April 4, 1968,
you were assassinated.

Was it the Government?
Was it the CIA?
Was it the FBI?
Was it just a guy?

We will never know.

The only thing we know
and remember,
is that you were,
are and will always be,
the King.

"Padre Pio"

I've had a dream
about you twice.

I have seen you
during sleep
paralysis
and even heard
your voice.

You're still
fighting Satan,
on the hills of
Pietrelcina,
while I'm still
a mortal here
in this distorted
dimension.

I wish I was
in your dimension,
I wish I could
confess with you.

I've been bad.

As you,
I did not give
my life to God
at the age of 10.

As you,
I did not
have stigmata

on my body.

But I still
believe
in mysticism
and in you,
with devotion.

I know, you look
upon me.

I believe that
you can bi-locate,
because you are in
heaven and you
are here with me.

The smell
of flowers,
still comes out of
your wounds.

I was able to smell it
when I visited your
lonely cell
and I can
smell it now.

You died in 1968,
but you never died
and in that
same year
you were
re born into
eternity.

At 2:30 am,
on the day of
your departure,
you asked for
Jesus and Mary
and you were
granted Paradise.

You are still alive
in the flesh,
in the soul
and in the
holy spirit.

"James Cook"

The Endeavour,
is still navigating
and HMS Resolution,
is still aground on
the Great Barrier Reef.

Your name is
everywhere,
you were
and are,
the greatest
navigator,
explorer,
commander
and cartographer
of all time.

The Royal Navy,
the three voyages
into the unknown,
their resonance,
can still be heard.

One day,
from the
Bay of Despair,
you went far,
into the open sea,
until you found
Terra Australis,
the incognito.

On your final

trip, Resolution
and Discovery
traveled to the
Hawaiians Islands,
where tension arose.

You died.

First they thought
you were Lono,
then their enemy.

You died
a brutal death,
but HMS Resolution
is still sailing
far and away,
in an immense
ocean of memories,
sounds, images
and you Captain.

"Winston Churchill"

"You cannot reason
with a tiger,
when your head
is in its mouth".

1940,
the Roaring Lion,
against Adolf.

A war meant
to be lost,
but won against
all odds.

Spitfires,
Hurricanes,
Messerschmitts
and the
Nazi War Machine,
above our skies,
while you,
yes you,
who looked
like a baby,
were sipping
a cup of earl Grey tea
calmly and gently.

The meeting with the
Generals did
not go well.

All against you,

all against war
and all for peace
negotiations.

Only you believed
in the serious
war machine
that Britain was.

Against all odds,
with air superiority
and advanced
technologies,
you brought a
nation to fight
"in France,
on the streets
and on the beaches."

And you,
with that chubby
baby face,
no hair,
won against
"that maniac,"
who wanted
the Blitz to be
a final move
toward
colonization
of a famous
colonizer.

England is not
property
of the Nazi regime

and the Gestapo
will never
be present
on British soil.

You achieved
the impossible,
you were
and are England.

"Execution day"

Dear God
the day has come,
my senses
are so sharp,
I can detect
the flight of a fly
and all of its movements
in slow motion.

The guards come
and I get up,
my legs are shaking.

Because of
the excitement,
I urinate in my pants.

Funny,
the guards
make me wash
and change.

This is the last
time I wash.

I will miss you water,
I will miss you soap.

Will I miss everything?
Or will I be ok
in the underworld?
The guards do a
full search on me,

as if I was hiding
something,
in this maximum
security place.

They put me
in chains,
grab me by
both my arms.

I look at them,
at their profiles,
If they could only feel
what I am
feeling now.

They do not
look at me,
they don't say
a word to me,
only a few commands.

No tears come
out of my eyes,
I am surprised
about this,
there is really
no need to cry.

I'm about to
meet my creator.

We walk at
a slow pace,
in a very
bright corridor.

I can see the walls,
they are so
white and clean.

A priest follows us.

The walls
of the corridor
become narrower
and narrower.

I'm a walking
dead, my friends.

My God, this
corridor is never-ending.

I finally convince my self,
that I'm about to die,
for a crime
I have committed
a few years ago.

They think I did it.

In reality, I didn't.

I am paying for
someone else's crime
and it's ok with me.

I accept the punishment.

We finally arrive
in a very bright room,
that looks like

a hospital room.

They put me
on a weird chair,
on which I am bound.

They start preparing
the lethal injection.

I'm now a resting dead.

Soon I will die,
soon I will find out
about the reign of God,
Purgatory, or Hell.

While my life passes
by in my head like a movie
and just a few seconds
away from dying, a phone
call arrives.

My life has
been spared.

Visualize the
expression
on my face.

"Workplace"

8am,
the only sound
comes from emails arriving
in the hundreds,
a phone call
now and then,
then silence again.

The atmosphere is full
of adrenaline, something
is about to explode in here.

Within a few minutes,
the butchers, the rats,
the pigs, the snakes
will fill this workplace.

9am.

Here they come,
the office becomes
a butchery, a war field,
with land mines all over the place,
an octagon to fight with bare hands
and bare feet.

The show begins,
arms and legs start flying,
bad words in the air,
punches, bites fill up
the innocence of this place.

The first match ends!

Break!

Next match begins!
There is so much greed,
there is so much individualism,
egos are huge.

Darwin should be proud
of his Natural Selection
and his struggle of the fittest.

Suddenly,
the end of the day arrives,
the end of the match is here.

All the white collar animals
go away.

There is peace now in the office.

No more blood to spill.

There is silence,
occasionally the sound of a new email,
sometimes the phone rings
and the non-stop noise of the server
fills the air.

"The Asteroid"

Between Mars and Jupiter,
there is a beautiful
display of precious stones.

They are suspended
in a circle of death,
orbiting the
next victims.

Further out,
the Kuiper Belt
can be found.

A much larger display
of precious
orbiting stones.

Within these
two belts,
our fate, the
fate of our
beautiful planet,
is already sealed.

It could happen today,
tomorrow,
or in 1 million years.

Our name is embedded
on one of these stones
and one day
this stone,
will change

its trajectory.

It will come
out of the belt
and it will shoot toward us.

This has happened
many times
in the history
of our planet.

There have been
many near misses.

We are living
on borrowed time.

These thoughts
make me think
how everything
trivial really is.

These thoughts
actually make me
appreciate life
even more.

Therefore
I wish to witness
the event
in my lifetime.

"Matryoshka doll"

This is the
age of dating.

Everybody is
dating everyone.

Once online dating
was discovered,
the frenzy of selfies begun.

This is the age of "me,"
the age of narcissism,
the age of the fake news.

I show to the world
what I am not,
I lie to the world.

This is the age of lies
and of the multiple
personality disorder.

This reminds me of
the Matryoshka dolls.

Our inner personalities,
in this era, are infinite.

We dig and dig,
to create characters
of fiction.

We have lost our way,
we have lost our self.

The term human
is not to be used any-more.

We have become post-humans,
with many personalities.

We are possessed by
our self.

The problem
is so big,
that there is
no turning back.

We are part of the
so-called
internet of things.

Today we
are one thing,
tomorrow we are
another thing.

If a Matryoshka doll
had 99 smaller
dolls in it,
we would be
doll number 99.

We have reached
the bottom.

If we could only
go back to doll 1,
the real us,
things would be
much better
and simpler.

Everything is so
complicated,
we are a
Matryoshka doll.

"Abnormal wave"

I find myself
in the middle of the ocean,
far from the coast,
floating without
precise destination.

This is not my environment,
I'm not sure what's lurking
under my feet.

I am not able
to see the bottom,
I can see only
a pitch dark blue solitude
and some silhouettes passing by,
once in a while.

I'm afraid,
I'm expecting that
bite any moment
or just to be dragged
into the abyss.

All of a sudden,
on the line of the horizon,
I see an immense wave
coming toward me.

The wave travels at high speed
and it's really tall.

What do I do?
Do I escape?

There is nowhere to run to,
I patiently await my faith.

I'm not sure,
what's going to happen to me,
once the wave arrives.

My mind is numb,
I'm cold, in shock
and still waiting
for that inevitable
bite on my legs.

The wave is coming,
fear turns into interest,
amusement.

After all,
I'm in God's country,
I'm in his hands.

I should never be afraid
of the unknown,
I should be strong,
I should be courageous
because God is with me.

The wave hits me hard;
I go underwater;
It's beautiful;
It's so blue;
I can see a few lights
at the bottom.

I run out of oxygen,
but all of a sudden

oxygen doesn't
matter any-more
and it's all so pristine
and amazing.

"Seven capital sins"

In my book:
luxuria becomes castitas;
gula becomes temperantia;
avaritia becomes caritas;
acedia becomes industria;
ira becomes patientia;
invidia becomes humanitas;
and superbia becomes humilitias.

Once in my life,
I fell into the grip of lust.
I had everything,
I had the impossible.
Now, just like
San Francesco,
I wear cheap
leather sandals
and I work the land,
with bare hands,
to obtain its fruits.
I personally go to Haiti,
to take these fruits
to the poorest of the
poorest.

Once in my life,
I've eaten to the
point of exploding.
All the foods in my
pantry, kitchen
and fridge has
now been sent,
special delivery,

to Caracas, Venezuela.
Once in my life,
I said, "Greed is good."
I have now donated all
of my money,
to the people of
the Democratic
Republic of Congo.
They live on one dollar
per day.

Once in my life,
sloth knocked on
my door and gave
me the gift of
oversleeping.
I now only sleep
4 hours per night.
I must get up early,
every morning.
I'm building a new church,
in Zimbabwe,
the land of blood
diamonds.

Once in my life,
wrath came to
exchange with me
few words.
It was the wrath
of God in person.
Instead of shouting,
I now sing beautifully,
songs of love and
humanity to dying
patients in hospitals

in Burundi.
I am not afraid of
the civil war.

Once in my life,
I felt envy when
a friend of mine
bought a house
much bigger
than mine.
I have sold my house,
burnt the money,
to celebrate Eritrea,
an Italian colony
in the 19th century,
that has never
recovered economically
since then.

Once in my life,
I was overconfident,
and very arrogant.
I now love my new me,
I'm into modesty
and my heart is full of
Humanity. I went
to Afghanistan,
opened a non-profit
industry, to help the
35% unemployed.

Life is now a miracle!

"How to be a man"

A1,
lesson 1,
page 1,
chapter 1:
"How to be a man."

A real man values
chastity. A real man
only has one woman
for his entire life.

A real man,
refrains from deviant
sexual conduct.

A real man has
temperance.

If you punch
this man on the face,
he will show
your forgiveness
and humanity.

A real man is
devoted to charity,
benevolence.

A real man is
an altruist,
because
"Deus Caritas Est."

This man thrives
on generosity.

A real man loves
diligence, hard
work, dedication
and strong work
ethics. Laziness
is not on the menu.

This man wakes up
with the rooster
at 5am.

A real man
knows what
patience is.

This man
morals are
based on mercy.

He never looses
his calm.

A real man,
is happy to
see people
around him,
being successful.

This man
never desires
other's possessions.

A real man
is made of
bravery
and modesty.

This man never
shows pride.

He keeps his
success to his
heart forever.

This is what a
real man,
or a superman is.

"Eva and Adolf, a love story"

The storm of war,
the hurricane
of the machine guns.

Nothing can
separate us,
not even the
Red Army,
nor the star
up in the sky.

Not even Winston,
can say no to
our partnership.

Our love is meant
to go on history books,
our love is meant to
exist forever.

No one has to know
what happens,
when at night
we go to our room,
at the Berghof.

It's our secret.

Our relationship,
will be sealed forever
under Berlin.

Our fate is written
and the bitter truth,
will be the
end of our
lives on this earth.

Eternal in
the underworld
and in the afterlife,
we'll meet
again soon.

For now,
a bullet silences me,
cyanide murders you.

You stayed with me
until the end,
faithful as God,
loyal as a wife
should be,
we became
the most famous
couple on earth.

"Learning how not to miss you"

It is so impossible
to achieve this,
it feels like walking on an
oily surface.

You struggle to walk,
fall on the oily floor
and cannot advance.

I do miss you very much,
I wish that with magic,
I could be with you,
within a blink of an eye
or with science,
using teleportation.

I am a scientist,
working on a
teleportation
machine.

The prototype
is almost ready.

I need a test subject.

For love,
I will test this
machine on me,
because I must
get to you,
no matter what.

So I get into
the device,
I set all
the parameters
and the arrival's
coordinates.

I press the button.

BAMF!

I'm gone,
in a fraction of a
second.

Something
goes wrong,
and at the
end I never
get to you.

I'm stocked
in a parallel
reality.

It feels like
being in a glass jar.

From inside this jar,
I can see you,
but you can't see me.

It is so true,
love makes you do,
crazy things.

"Evil"

The absence of good,
generosity,
empathy
and God,
is evil.

The chief commander,
in charge of spreading this evil,
is the fallen angel,
the northern star.

His life,
is all about the 7
capital sins.

Evil is the antagonist,
in the story of life.

Being evil,
means many things,
the spectrum is really broad,
from killing an ant,
to killing a man.

Is there any difference?

It is true,
that society of today,
loves and asks only for evil.

The good things,
are for the weak.

Society wants
to spill blood.

Black is better than white,
gray is more interesting then pink,
red is sexual,
an aphrodisiac.

There is only a minority of
people that believe in Good.

There is no money in good,
there is no future in good,
however, still, the ways
of God are better than
the means of the beast.

"On your grave"

I compare
my father,
to the English
explorer,
James Cook or to the
Spanish conquistador
Hernan Cortez.

Both men, with
great dreams
and goals,
with a lot
of discipline.

My father died
a few years ago,
but he is still here
with me.

Sometimes it feels
like he is
in my room.

So I talk to him.

It is a therapy
and the illusion
that he is
still alive,
is like winning
a lottery.

Today, I'm

at his place,
his tomb.

On his tomb,
I leave my tears,
my aura,
my energy,
my dreams
and my essence.

Every time
I'll have an
out of the
body experience,
I will visit
his tomb.

I promise.

"Washed ashore"

My ship came
down hard.

I was swallowed
by the ocean,
in a matter
of seconds.

The reason,
unknown.

I am all broken,
floating.

I am looking at
the sky.

The sun is right
on top of me.

I am waiting
for a shark bite,
which should
happen any
moment.

These waters
are known
to be infested
with bull sharks
and who knows,
probably even
by the Kraken.

A strong current,
takes me to a desert island.

It is a tiny island,
so small, I can see
the opposite shore,
from where I'm at.

I spend about 2 hours,
laying on this pristine
beach.

Getting desperate,
will not help.

All of a sudden,
I spot a small box
washed ashore.

It is made of wood
and nicely carved.

I open it, inside
there is a
letter that says,
"Hope never dies."

"Optimism and pessimism"

Optimism said
to pessimism,
what are we
fighting for?

Why are we
resembling
2 gunslingers,
in the wild west?

Why do we
hate each other?
Why the lack
of balance?

Pessimism replied:
It is not as easy
as it looks,
to join forces
and to create
a better world.

Once I was
like you,
but with
the years,
I turned dark.

I was forced to
turn dark.

It would have
been you
or myself.
You see in life,
there's always
a constant battle
between
evil and
good.

All I can
promise you,
because I
can foresee the
Future, is
that one day,
you and I will
become a
gradient of
intense colours,
because of a
revolution in
men's heart
is about to
happen.

"Beings from another dimension"

Messages started
arriving 1 year ago.

Messages in binary code,
Morse code and
in every other system.

The messages
are now
coming in
every day,
every minute.

These messages,
are messages of
complexity.

"The kids are
playing with
the matches,"
they say.

The messages
come from
beings or
people of the future,
that have been there,
that have seen it all.

We are the ants,
they are the
Colossus.

We are the slime,
they are grace.

So much to learn,
so little time.

We need to go,
we need to finally go,
where man has never been.

We need to save
our human species.

Do we need to?
According to God,
we need to preserve
ourselves.

According to nature,
we can't stop
evolution and the
natural flows of
everything.

Messages come
that contain,
engineering plans
to build a ship.

We build it.

We are not that
stupid after all.

The ship's name is
"Transcend."

Today we go.

Today we transcend.

Today we move to the next step.

Today we change everything.

Today we become a legend.

"From far away"

While I was in
a profound sleep,
last night,
I was dreaming
really strange
things.

At a certain point,
in my dream,
I was walking
in a dark
street,
all alone.

This is the full story,
in the present tense.

100 meters away
from me,
I see tiny
moving lights,
made of many
colours.

These lights
get closer
and closer
to me.

Suddenly
I see shapes.

Three men
or humanoids.

No features on
their faces,
just moving
tiny multi-colour lights,
under a transparent
thin skin.

They wear
no clothes,
they have
no hair.

They look like mannequins.

I am now
in front of them,
they have no eyes,
no mouths,
no noses.

I can hear them in my mind.

They use telepathy
and simply say to me:
"Come with us" and
"Don't be afraid."

"Fast as an eagle"

God designed me.

God wanted this for me.

I have a vast wingspan
and a yellow beak.

I am faster
as a bullet train.

My sight
allows me
to see every
dimension.

I am free
and I know how to
provide for myself.

As a matter of fact
I am the best hunter
the world has ever seen.

But I am sad and
devastated.

An awful animal
called Man,
is destroying
our beautiful
blue marble planet.

This animal
is not concerned
about the trees,
not concerned
about the rivers
and not concerned
about the mountains.

This animal
is greedy,
irresponsible,
dirty and jealous.

This animal
does not know
what the meaning
of love is.

So tears
come down
on my beak,
day and night.

Mother nature
is protesting,
but Man cannot
or does not want to
see this.

Mother Nature
is being ignored.

The end
will not be nice
unless Man
becomes a true
son of Mother Nature.

"Silence Universe Style"

I close my eyes,
It's late at night.

I lay flat on the grass.

After a while,
I open my eyes
and breath slowly.

I see the Universe,
I immediately feel
the insignificance
of my existence.

I think of the
Hubble Telescope,
all alone, so far
away from home.

I can only imagine
and picture in my mind,
the remote places
the telescope sees.

In those places,
the sound has
to be so profound,
that it must
assume other forms,
forms we just
can't understand.

That silence,

in my imagination,
is made of an immense darkness,
violent events
and lights we've
never seen before.

Not even Hubble
makes any noise,
in the immense
and remote
vacuum of space.

I can't compare this silence,
to anything here on Earth.

I think about it,
it's like a therapy
and it feels alive,
lights of years
away from me.

I'm a dot.

"Sleep Paralysis"

When time is no more
and when senses are lost,
something or someone
gently embraces me
and does not let go,
in my room,
in the middle
of the night.

For a few minutes or hours,
who knows, I enter
the 6th dimension,
in which there
is no oxygen,
in which there
is no sound,
therefore no words
come out of my mouth,
not even noise
when I try to scream.

This dimension
might be the
deep darkness
of space.

While I am incapacitated,
stupefied
and of course
amused by all this,
I must be awake.

It cannot be that I am asleep,

cause everything seems so real,
but so scary.

This event has happened
to me so many times,
to the point that
it makes me think,
I must be a mad man!

It is so scary,
it reminds me of death,
it reminds me
of a black widow
hunting and
catching prey.

I feel like prey exactly,
I feel disabled,
incapacitated,
vulnerable to
whatever force
of this world
or another,
comes into
my room to get me.

"Quiet as the future"

The year cannot be told,
because in the future
the concept of
time has changed.

The year is an
extremely
long number
and the human
species has changed,
we have evolved
into something,
not into someone.

The future is
white, crisp,
aseptic, clean,
too bright
and everything
has an order.

Everything is a part of a
more extensive system.

In this so well
organized future,
I can reach the sky,
watch the future
passing by from above.

From up here,
the wind,
the colour

of the clouds
makes me feel
the desolation
of this new era.

Is it a Technological Era?

We do not know any-more,
we might have
become technology.

The future is infinite,
it will never end
and we, beings of
light or perhaps
a new form
of humans beings,
are here to stay forever.

We are here in the
clouds, observing
the white, crisp
and a bright
future from above.

"Alpheratz"

You are the brightest,
the most beautiful star
within the constellation
of Andromeda.

You are not alone,
you have a sister
or a brother orbiting
around you.

You were chosen
by different star races,
to become a livable planet.

This has happened
a few billion years ago.

Now you are a lonely star again,
with your only and true friend.

Many light years separate us,
but I wonder how it would be,
to be there.

All that silence
and you two,
two majestic
free spirits,
in a free Cosmo.

You'll be there for a few
billion years more,
you and your lonely friend,

chasing you
and worshiping your
brightness.

"Special skills"

They teach you
to be critical,
analytical, creative
and innovative.

Then they tell you
to be flexible
and dependable,
you got to be
adaptable, dynamic
and competent.

Another crucial thing
society wants,
is a problem solver.

You have to be
a decision maker,
insightful
and intuitive.

You must have
interpersonal skills,
always respectful,
collaborative,
you have to be able
to build relationships.

Another important thing,
you have to be motivated,
dedicated, you
must have energy,
you got to be

a hard worker,
you must be
ethical at work
and in society.

You got to be
programmed,
a slave.

My skills are different:
I love nature,
I love the mountains,
the stars,
the oceans,
dogs and cats,
I love to paint,
to draw,
to work with clay
and I do not
have a watch,
cause I work
on my own time.

I was born free,
I will die free.

"Mars"

The process of
terraforming Mars,
is finally over.

A thick ozone layer
is now protecting
the red planet.

Plants and trees
are everywhere.

The once hostile
and dry planet
is now a paradise.

Our beloved earth
is under threat.

It seems like the
devil won the
battle against Christ.

Governments are
preparing the evacuation
to our new home.

We are on a Spaceship
called "The Ark."

It's like being in
a science fiction movie.

We arrive at the

Mars colony,
after a very
long journey.

We are placed
in a particular building
for some sort
of rehabilitation,
due to the long trip.

The day comes
in which we
finally receive
our Mars permanent
residency card
and we're out.

We can breathe,
just like on earth.

We receive
the news that
millions of people
have just died on earth
due to the clime
changing continuously.

Earth is at the
end of its life cycle.

We were
lucky to escape.

We are the
chosen ones.

Now we start
from scratch.

We are no
longer British,
Americans, Japanese,
we are now Martians.

"Love described by stellar dynamics"

I have no other ways
to talk about love,
I have exhausted
all of my resources,
to explain what this
thing called love is.

I will try to refresh
the subject by using
stellar dynamics.

According to stellar dynamics,
love is considered to be a star,
a celestial object
found all over
the Universe.

This star moves
in mysterious ways,
it moves according
to the dynamics and laws
of Outer space.

These laws, we cannot
yet understand.

What we understand is
the gravitational
field that love creates,
just like a star.

Love moves thanks to
mutual gravity

against another body.

So while stellar dynamics
describe this mutual gravity,
celestial mechanisms
can be used
to explain movements
and trajectories
of love in outer space.

Finally the
interaction between
galaxies, can
explain the turbulence
and disturbances
of love against
another body.

Love is maths,
physics, chemistry,
astrophysics,
dynamics, and
much more.

Love is also Humanity.

"Being humans"

Not yet running
on Elysian fields,
not yet dust
in the wind.

But alive
and kicking,
we humans
are kids,
living on
this playground.

Being humans,
means being stubborn,
with shiny eyes,
conquering everything,
before falling into
the Pyriphlegethon or the
Acheron.

Being humans
also means love
and compassion,
not only for
our friends,
but also for
Nature.

On the
first day of our life,
we are already
presented with a
bill, with a

debt to pay.

On the same
day, we are given to
our mother
and to Death,
which day after day
will make subtractions.

Being human
means watching
life passing by,
without really
understanding
a thing.

I remind my self,
that what is
really worth
in this life is
watching, learning,
crying, loving,
smiling, kissing
and listening to
"God saves the queen."

In eternity.

"The age of races"

We are at the verge
of historical changes.

The information age,
is already weaving
goodbye to us.

The information is
becoming already
integrated in
our fabric of life.

The new age is going
to be the age of
faster data,
faster connections,
faster everything.

It now takes only a
few seconds to
look for something.

Soon, information
will exist within us.

Our bodies will be
fused with technologies.

We are going to
be the technologies,
or at least, our body
will be directly interfaced
with the technologies.

Humans will also be
replaced by the
newest and
fastest humans,
an augmented
version of us.

There will be
a massive leap in
human evolution.

It will be
an artificial
evolution,
forced by us.

There is now
a race to destroy
human civilization
and a race to
create the new us.

This is humans playing God.

"Different types of love"

In our life, we
are not able
to understand
what love is.

Love might be
an entity like
Cupid, or love might
be the Devil itself.

Love could be energy,
or love might be a virus.

According to the
various emotional
blows that love can
cause to an
individual, we can
perhaps identify
few different types
of this thing called
love.

Love is based on the
following things: sex, calm,
storm, patience and murder.

Love is sex, when
gravity is so intense,
that two bodies,
must touch
each other,
in an eternal

boxing match.

Love is calm when
hair turns blue or silver
and it seems like
nothing changes.

Love is a storm,
when you make every
possible mistake in your life
and particularly
when you persevere
in making those mistakes.

Love is patience,
when it has just blossomed,
when everything
is fresh and you're
waiting for that first contact,
that first kiss.

Finally, love is murder,
when one is so heartbroken,
because of the actions of his
or her lover,
that the only
solution is
an overdose.

"The mental illness era"

We are supposed
to be, in the
information era,
transitioning into
the artificial
intelligence era,
but all I see,
is augmented
mental illness.

Men and women,
under the knife,
to get fake muscles,
fake noses, chins
and brains.

A woman in the
US married a tree.

A man married a horse.

Another man has sex
with his car.

Kids jump from
one building
to another,
in a strange game
of Russian roulette.

Men that are girls,
girls that are men,
asexual individuals,

androgynous
boys and girls,
who want to
resemble aliens.

Companies spending
billions, to go to Mars,
while billions of
kids die of
starvation year
after year.

We have lost our ways.

We are unrecognizable
to ourselves.

Technology supposed to bring
prosperity and equality.

But this is not the case
any more and the spaces
between us get wider
and wider.

We have transitioned
into the mental
illness era.

"The battle within us"

The Nazi machine
is advancing
toward us.

I am afraid,
I might
not see my love
never again,
if we fall to the
Gestapo hands.

I hold my rifle
very tightly,
I get ready.

I close my
eyes for a
moment, I imagine
how Europe would
be without Hitler.

It is a beautiful
image, for a
brief moment.

All of a sudden,
we see, from
our improvised
bunker,
the Germans.

They are probably

more scared
then us, but
have promised
to their dictator,
to win
this battle.

They are now
in front of us
and we can't fire
a single bullet.

They are just
kids in uniform.

They are crying
and shaking.

They have seen us.

We drop the rifles,
we lose our helmets,
we throw away
the extra ammunition,
they do exactly
the same.

We run toward
each other
and fall into
an embrace
of tears and hope.

There is fear,
but hope,
that the tyranny

will end.

We run away
from the battlefield.

We hide in
the mountains.

"Genesis"

Genesis is
finally here.

The year is
irrelevant, it is
a date in the white
and crisp future,
in which,
the biological
evolution
has stopped.

Genesis is my
lover, until the
end of my life.

I am a genius,
I built her.

She's got a
biological brain,
made of cells,
created in a
very white
and clean lab.

She is the
real deal,
a replicant,
indistinguishable
from a human.

We were at the

point of becoming
augmented humans.

We became that.

Then the
new era started.

This era is
the era of trans
biological humans.

In this era,
everything is possible
and the future runs at the
speed of light.

She is mine, and only
faithful to me,
because she has been
engineered this way.

If some other
men touches her,
or violates her,
a cascading
destructive event
will occur.

Her bio-tech
body will be no more,
but her brain
will survive and
will be uploaded
into the cube,
a safe place for

augmented souls.

And when my
life will come
to an end,
my brain will also
be uploaded into the cube.

I will meet Genesis
again, not in this world.

I will meet her
in the new world,
the digital one.

"You should forgive me"

These sentences
are taken from
my personal inner
book of forgiving.

I speak from the heart.

Sometimes the past
of each one of us,
can be fatal,
can be a monster
with white eyes
and huge fangs.

The good news is
that today the sun
shines, today butterflies
are flying upon our heads.

We have all changed,
evolved into our new us.

We are better, bigger,
stronger, wiser.

Therefore I am going
to read a sentence
from my book of
forgiving,
I hope you'll like it.

Forgive me.

"Losing you Losing me"

I never thought
I could be lost,
I never thought
I could be wrong.

I don't want to know
if you're with
somebody else,
cannot imagine
how I would feel like.

In this very moment I can say,
right now my mind dreams of you
coming back to me,
right now with 3 simple words,
I would change the way you feel,
right now I'm telling you,
what are we waiting for?

Have you got anything to say?

I'm losing you, like you're losing me,
can't you see? can't you feel my state?
All these words are blown away,
by the wind, by your silence.

And tomorrow, the silence,
the wind, your words,
all gone, forever
and ever.

"In my mind"

When I'm not with you,
when you're not with me,
I'm so powerless
and I'm all at sea.

I can touch my pain,
an open wound,
in my mind, in my
soul there you are.

In my mind, in my soul,
I am coming home.

The only way,
I'll find my space,
in this empty place,
I will keep on
coming back.

The only way,
I'll make you say,
that you want me still,
will you keep on
coming back?

If I'm not with you,
I cannot exist,
I will not insist.

I'll try to make it real,
you thought me
how to be so in love.

"If things happen for a reason"

If things happen for a reason,
tell me the reason why
I'm losing you.

Things happen suddenly,
without any explanation at all.

I still get up in the morning,
with this pain in my chest.

You and I reside,
you and I reside, in my soul.

If things happen for a reason,
let it be this way.

I try to justify
every single thing,
every day.

You and I reside,
you and I reside
in my soul.

I don't want to
lose my faith in you,
I just want
a brand new start,
a new life, with you, so cool,
with you, so cool.

If things happen for a reason,
learn as much as you can.

If things happen
without any sense,
someone has
got a plan for you,
because you and I reside,
you and I live in my heart.

"From minor perturbation to a Tornado"

I should have
seen this coming,
instead, I made
the same mistakes
that I have repeated
over and over again
during my entire life.

I got with the
wrong persons again,
I lost everything again,
I lost my balance again
and I lost my eyes
and hands again.

What is it that makes
me graduating from life
with a major in catastrophes?

I don't know.

I am probably looking
in the wrong places,
everything is
wrong all the time.

Everything is
sad all the time.

Sometimes I think
I was a mistake,
but all of a sudden
I get illuminated

by a higher entity,
which reminds me
that we are only
humans after all!

"Time"

What we
were yesterday,
is different from
what we are today
and tomorrow.

Our body
regenerates
itself, up to
the bones.

Time and biological
natural processes
are unstoppable forces.

If these forces
change us
second by second,
what happens
to our soul?
Does it change as well?

And if the process
of aging can be
altered or stopped,
what are we
going to
evolve into?

We are not what
we think we are.

We can't see

what happens
inside us,
we have
no control.

If a natural
catastrophe,
does not stop
humanity, then
these forces will
continue to
work inside us
and will create
a new dominant species.

I dream about this,
I have visions of a
crisp, clean,
future, where
everything
is quiet
and white,
where desolation
prevails
and where a
new version
of us exists.

Time is the
only thing
that will
never change,
but time
changes us.

"The true meaning of being in love"

Love should be
a sublime thing,
love should be
mystical
and bizarre.

Love should
take you from
the bottom of the
Mariana Trench,
to the peak of K2.

Love should
surpass the
100 km
atmosphere
and take you
to outer space,
for a sweet ride
and gently
get you back
and safe on our
blue marble ball.

Love should be
a doctor that
fixes you and
it should also be
the nurse that
feeds you and
cleans you if
and when you are sick.

Love is the 3rd wave,
a wave that
can be nice,
and gentle
for beginner
surfers.

But love is
also the
tsunami that
destroys
nuclear power
plants.

Love is
a sparrow,
love is a hawk.

Love is life
and love is death.

Love is a duality,
and its made of logic.

Love is a singularity,
a black hole,
capable of
devouring you.

"A bye bye kiss, not a good bye kiss"

I just woke up,
I imagine drinking
a really nice cup of coffee.

My imagination runs
wild for a moment,
before I get ready
to go to the jungle city.

It's another day
in paradise city.

On my side, my lover,
my sleeping beauty,
sleeping like a
big fat cat.

I get up, slowly
and quietly.

I do not want to
wake her
up this time.

I will make it, she
will still be
sleeping, while I go.

While I get up
gently and slowly,
she grabs my arm,
for the usual
goodbye kiss routine.

It's not really
a goodbye,
it's only a lovely
bye, bye.

No matter how
careful I am,
she sleeps with
an opened eye.

She must have
that kiss in the
morning, to
start the engines.

Finally I understand,
that she's here
to stay, therefore,
this is not a
goodbye kiss,
it's a sweet bye,
bye kiss.

Printed in Poland
by Amazon Fulfillment
Poland Sp. z o.o., Wrocław

54117285R00215